Total **Scrapbooking**

Sarah Mason and Karen McIvor

MQP

Contents

Foreword
Scrapbooking in the 21st Century

Scrapbooking is not a new craft; it has been with us since the Victorian era when mementos and keepsakes were pasted into notebooks. The new technology of photography was also occasionally included, but the main emphasis tended to be upon recording events, stories, thoughts, and memories. As fashions changed and the pace of life increased, this hobby gradually faded into obscurity.

During the latter part of the twentieth century, a resurgence of interest in researching genealogy and recording family history brought with it a renewed interest in scrapbooks. Modern scrapbooks are an exciting way to record the everyday history of our lives. They are not just about the "big" events such as births, weddings, and celebrations; scrapbooks also provide the opportunity to record the people, places, and things that are meaningful to us.

Although modern technology such as digital photography and computers can be incorporated into scrapbooks, they are still basically about telling your story and leaving a legacy. How sad is it to find a pile of old family photographs and not know who the people are? Photograph albums are all well and good but are often only interesting when someone takes the time to talk about the story behind the picture. Take the opportunity to create a scrapbook and leave a legacy that will be so much more than a family heirloom.

Karen & Sarah

Opposite: This beautiful scrapbook was created by the photographer's mother and is a treasured record of their family history.

Below: Albums come in a variety of sizes, and you can make your own in any size.

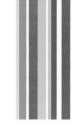

Introduction

Almost every one of us has a box, bag, or drawer full of photographs that is being added to all the time. Memories of family holidays, birthday parties, and afternoons in the garden stay wrapped in their packaging or slide around over one another becoming a jumbled mess. Purchasing film and developing photographs can be expensive, particularly if we then do nothing with them. If our pictures are not protected and preserved, they will rapidly begin to fade, crack and deteriorate. More importantly, the opportunities to find out about and record the stories behind these photographs can quickly pass us by and before we know it, our children or grandchildren will be presented with a box of unknown faces.

The same can be said of digitally stored images. They take up little space, but then again, they are hidden away on discs, memory cards, and computers, rarely to be seen. It is not unknown for discs to be damaged or computers to crash and these precious memories to be lost forever.

This book will provide you with the inspiration to create your own scrapbook pages regardless of your level of crafting experience. The first part of the book offers a host of techniques with step-by-step instructions that clearly show how to create some fabulous effects for your projects. We have also included some example pages illustrating ways in which these techniques can be incorporated into beautiful scrapbook pages.

The second half of the book is full of inspiration for themed scrapbook layouts. Each section has full instructions for double and single page designs that will be sure to ignite a spark of creativity. Our talented designers offer a range of styles, so there is sure to be something for everyone. We show you how to combine products, papers and pictures to create pages that help to tell your stories.

Scrapbooking is such a wonderful craft, it brings families and like-minded people together to create lasting legacies for future generations. We hope that you enjoy this book as much as we have enjoyed creating it and are inspired to make a scrapbook that will become a family treasure.

Techniques

scissors

eyelet hammer

tweezers

Glue pen

craft knife and cutting mat

eyelet kit

archival pen

hole piercer

setting mat

pencil and eraser

metal ruler

trimmer

Getting Started

Scrapbooking is the presentation of photographs and memories in an environment that will protect and preserve them. It is also a fun, creative way to store your family photographs while telling your story to future generations. Creating a scrapbook is so much more than putting together a photograph album – values, traditions, feelings, and heritage can all be collected together and passed on through these beautiful pages.

This paper craft is far from new. It has in fact been with us for many years, reaching its peak with the Victorians, who created beautiful collections of photographs, newspaper clippings, greeting cards, and souvenirs. General crafters are now rediscovering the opportunities that scrapbooking provides to create something meaningful and special for future generations. With very few "rules" to follow, virtually any other craft can be incorporated into scrapbook page design. More and more needle workers, card makers, and painters are discovering scrapbooking, and finding something else within the craft: the chance to make something that will tell their stories on their behalf.

Scrapbooking has an additional attraction for people with an interest in genealogy. Family trees and stories can be recorded in an album together with pictures, photographs, and other material. There can be no better way to bring the past to life than a single source book that will act as a reference for all the family.

Essential tools

The basic tools required for scrapbooking are very similar to those needed for other paper crafts. They include a paper trimmer, craft knife, metal ruler, and self-healing cutting mat (see Chapter 2); an eyelet kit comprising a punch, setter, mat, and hammer (see Chapter 4); and a journaling pen, pencil, scissors, and eraser (see Chapter 6). You will also need a selection of adhesives, both wet and dry, as outlined in Chapter 2.

Your photographs

The focus of scrapbook pages should be the photographs. Many of us have boxes, drawers, or bags full of photographs of many different generations of our family and friends. All photographs will deteriorate if not properly protected, since temperature, humidity, and atmospheric pollutants can all ruin your treasured pictures. Some commercially available photograph albums will actually accelerate the degrading process, resulting in brown, brittle, and faded photographs. If you are unsure how safe your old albums are, carefully check the pages. Are they discoloring? Are they the "magnetic-cling" type? Has the adhesive discolored? Are your photos falling out of the album? If you can answer "Yes" to any of these questions, your album is probably unsafe for your pictures.

All is not lost, however, since you can remove your photographs from these albums and rescue them. If the adhesive proves difficult to remove, there are a number of products that quickly and gently soften and remove residue adhesive while protecting your photos.

When you have rescued your pictures from the boxes, or drawers, the next step is to sort through them. This will give you an opportunity to group or categorize the photographs, and also to choose the best pictures you have – the ones you want to put into a scrapbook NOW!

Torn, scratched, or otherwise damaged photographs can be given a new lease of life by a photo lab or through the use of photo-editing software. Heirloom images can be scanned and reproduced for scrapbooking if the original is too precious to use.

Changing an image into black and white or sepia can also produce some beautiful results and can address problems created by garish colors or wild patterns.

Scrapbooking may change the way you take your pictures. Perhaps you will take more pictures or will think a little more about how you take your photographs. Some scrapbookers develop a real passion for photography and develop this side of the hobby.

Opposite: Your toolbox will be added to as you progress.

Below: Printers are available to change the color of your images to black and white, or sepia tones, to help them fit in with your layout plans.

Cutting paper and card

One of the most frequently used cutting tools is a 12 in. (30 cm) paper trimmer. This can be in the form of a guillotine, a wheel cutter, or a sliding blade trimmer. You can perform the same tasks with a craft knife and ruler, but a trimmer makes cutting card and paper quick and easy. Many trimmers incorporate a folding ruler, which provides a handy method of ensuring accurate cutting; others offer the option of additional blades for fancy edges, scoring, and perforating. Many craft stores will allow you to try before you buy, allowing you to get the feel for how a particular trimmer works and establish whether or not it is compatible with your needs.

A craft knife, together with a metal ruler and self-healing cutting mat, are also scrapbooking essentials. Using these tools, you can create hand-cut titles and embellishments to make your scrapbook projects truly one of a kind. A craft knife is also a great tool if you want to do scrapbooking while away from home, as it is light and versatile, where some trimmers can be awkward and cumbersome. Craft knives are available with fixed and swivel blades. Many crafters find a fixed blade easier to manipulate, and this type of knife is also often cheaper. Rotary cutting wheels provide quick and easy cutting and are perfect for straight lines and larger curves, though not so good for cutting intricate details.

Size matters

The next step is to decide what size album you would like to use. There are a number of commercially available album sizes: 12 in. x 12 in., 8½ in. x 11½ in., 8 in. x 8 in., 7 in. x 5 in., and 6 in. x 6 in (30 cm x 30 cm, 21 cm x 28 cm, 20 cm x 20 cm, 18 cm x 13 cm, and 15 cm x 15cm). With so many options to choose from, the choice can be a little overwhelming. Most scrapbooking paper and card is produced in 12 in. x 12 in. or 8½ in. x 11½ in. (30 cm x 30 cm or 21 cm x 28 cm), and, as a result, most scrapbookers tend to choose one or other of these size albums. There are no rules in scrapbooking, though, and you can make your pages as large or as small as you like.

Although there is a wide range of beautiful albums available in a variety of colors and finishes, you might decide to make your own album to fit your own requirements. (A careful look at a scrapbook album will demonstrate how simple these are to produce yourself). A handmade album in an unconventional size can result in a unique and unusual project. Smaller albums are a great size for gifts, and their small scale means that they are often faster to put together.

If you would rather not put your work in an album, consider the other options. Pages can be professionally framed as a permanent memento and hung on the wall for all to admire. Frames are also available specifically for scrapbook page formats. These enable scrapbook pages to be displayed, and then quickly changed when your latest project is complete. A collection of twelve scrapbook pages can become a beautiful calendar, and a trip to a color photocopier means that all your family can enjoy your talents, every month.

In this book, you will find a treasure trove of ideas and inspiration for all levels. We focus on techniques that will help you to produce scrapbook pages you can feel proud of. Our designers will also show you how they used these techniques to produce beautiful layouts and projects for a wide range of themes and special occasions.

Opposite: Trimmers are an invaluable addition to your tool kit, and come to suit all budgets.

Below: There are myriad scissors and shears for tasks of different sizes as well as to create decorative edgings.

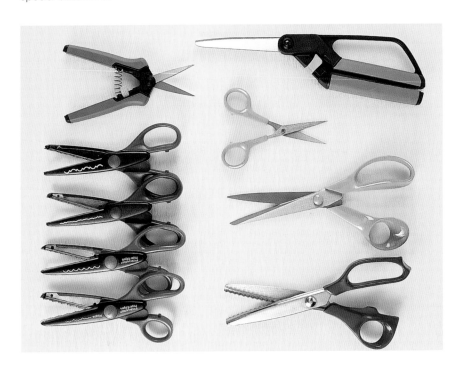

cropping mask

perspectives

craft-knife

self-healing cutting mat

metal ruler

m makingmemories

Composition

This is a term used to describe a group of principles related to visual design. In this chapter, we will focus on these principles – emphasis, balance, proportion, rhythm, and harmony – and highlight how you can use them to create great scrapbook pages that really "work."

These are not rules that must be strictly followed, and there is no "right" or "wrong" scrapbook composition. What one person finds visually pleasing, another will not – composition remains a matter of personal taste. Some truly great works of art break some or all of the guidelines for composition and are still highly acclaimed.

Every scrapbook page should have a focal point, something that catches your eye and makes you want to stay a while and really look at the page. When you gather together photographs for your pages, select one or two really strong images to highlight on the page; the remainder will reinforce the theme and create atmosphere. Creating emphasis in a composition can be achieved by cropping, framing, mounting, creating contrast, isolating an image, using size or grouping.

Cropping

This is one of the simplest ways to create a focal point. Cropping means to trim away some of the image to highlight the principal subject. The most common reason for cropping is when the subject of the photograph is off-center in the image. If you are unsure as to whether or not an image will be improved by cropping. Make a loose frame from two pieces of "L" shaped paper or card. As you increase, and decrease the size of the frame, you will quickly be able to see if the image requires cropping and by how

much. Mark the edge of the image to indicate the cutting line(s) before trimming the photograph with a paper trimmer or craft knife and ruler. Digital images can be cropped using photo-editing software to achieve the same results.

It is recommended that you scan and reprint very old pictures for which you do not have the negatives before cropping them, as mistakes can be tragic. Heritage photographs may be poorly composed, but the sections to be cropped could contain images of items of furniture or decorations that are historically interesting or "of the era." Cropping these away from the original photograph to emphasize the subject could mean that you lose a little piece of your history.

Mounting

This technique, known also as matting, is another way to draw the eye to your stronger images. Mark the shape of your photograph on a piece of card, then cut a ½ in. (12 mm) border around all four sides. The mount produces a visual frame for your picture, which adds emphasis. Create a double mount by attaching the mount to a second piece of card in a complementary or contrasting color and creating another border.

All the photographs on a page can be mounted, with the key pictures being double, triple, or even quadruple mounted to make a focal point. Vary the width of the mounts to produce interesting effects, or add interest through the choice of colored paper or card for your mounts. Textured papers or borders will have a similar effect.

Using size or grouping

In general terms, the larger the element, the more visual "weight" it has and the more it will draw the eye. If you do not have the option to use a large picture, try grouping pictures together. When several items are in close proximity to one another, they are perceived as one, rather than as individual elements.

Haute Couture

Great-great Grandmother

After I had asked around the family for old photographs, Doug's Mum came across this photo amongst a pile of family pictures. She told me that this was Nanny Duvall's Grandmother, which would make her Doug's great-great grandmother and Jack's great-great-great grandmother.

Framing

In the same way that a framed picture draws the eye, so framing a photograph on a scrapbook page creates emphasis. Cut a frame from card or paper and place this over your photograph. The frame can be used to mask unbalanced sections of your picture without the need to cut them off. Readymade frames are available from scrapbook stores in a range of colors, making framing your key pictures as easy as possible.

Symmetrical designs

The simplest way to produce visual balance is to make one page the mirror image of the other. This symmetrical approach will make sure that the pages complement each other and produce a quite static balance. This design works wonderfully with heritage pictures, since the formal poses of old studio shots cry out for solid, symmetrical balance. Try using this approach for other photographs such as portraits and weddings to produce a design that correlates to the style of the picture.

Asymmetrical designs

Double-page spreads can also be given a balanced design by using an asymmetrical approach, for example one large photograph can be balanced by two small ones. These designs are visually interesting and generate energy and dynamism. Make sure that the elements used in asymmetrical designs have the same visual weight in order to maintain the overall balance. Use this approach for informal photographs to create designs that add to the energy of the images.

Creating contrast

Another way of producing emphasis can be by using contrast. For example, one color picture used with a number of black-and-white images (or vice versa) will automatically draw the eye. A more subtle way of reinforcing the focal point of a picture is through isolation: leaving a small amount of space around a key image to emphasize its importance.

Proportion

The design principle of proportion relates to the placement of an element within a "frame." Whatever size scrapbook you work with, the background card or paper forms the "frame," and where you decide to attach your photographs can be significant to their overall impact. Try placing a focal-point picture off-center or in the page, as this is visually more interesting.

Balance

A balanced design will allow your eye to move across it easily, while an unbalanced design can be uncomfortable to view. Balance can be an important factor, particularly when designing double-page layouts, as each page should work with the other in an album.

Odd numbers

Another thing to be aware of when considering the principle of proportion is that odd numbers tend to work better visually than even ones. This principle is applied in all sorts of design areas, from flower arranging to painting. Repeat the same element on the page an odd number of times, and the design will tend to have a more "finished" look. Grouping odd numbers of different elements together suddenly makes them work visually, just like magic. Try this principle with your next project using photographs and embellishments to create a harmonious design quickly and simply.

Visual triangle

A design that has a good visual rhythm will allow the eye to move from one focal point to the next. There will be a flow to the work that makes it easy to look at.

The simplest way to create this rhythm is to create a visual triangle. This is another technique used in some of the best paintings. To understand the triangle, think of the human face. If you were presented with a picture of the eyes alone, you would probably look from one eye to the other, back and forth. This can be very tiring, as it does not allow the observer to rest. However, add in the nose and/or mouth, and suddenly the picture is very much easier to look at. This is the visual triangle in action, and it can be used in any orientation or size.

Haute couture

Designer: Karen McIvor
This page demonstrates the use of a single focal point.

Jack has tried to climb the Mountain Ash at the bottom of our garden for as long as we have lived here. It is such a big tree that it is difficult for anyone to climb into.

This summer he finally managed it and shouted for me to come and take some photos.

As I looked up at him through my viewfinder, it struck me once again how much nearer Jack is to becoming a young man. He was so determined to get up there, so focussed on his goal and so very proud of his achievement.

Climb high, Climb far, Your goal the sky, Your aim the stars

Climb as High

Designer: Karen McIvor

This double layout is almost completely symmetrical.

Risk going too far,
for only then can
you possibly find out
how far you can go.

There are 3 ways to
get to the top of a
tree:
1. sit on an acorn
2. make friends
   with a bird
3. climb it

Summer
2004

J

as you can dream

This close-up shows that there is another whole album within the layout on the previous page.

Triangles also tend to pull together the different elements on the page, whereas displaying items in pairs tends to separate them into sections. Photographs and embellishments can be used together to create a triangle on the page, allowing the eye to move from one element to the other.

Repetition

Create rhythm in your designs through repetition. Repeat colors, shapes, sizes, patterns, or textures, or try making the same shape with different patterns of paper to produce rhythm through two sources. Then reverse this concept and see if you can find the same texture in different shapes – this can be a really fun way to get creative. You could also try making different shapes in the same size.

Connections

When placing items on the page, try to make sure that every element has a visual connection with another element in the design. This link visually "grounds" each item, tying it to the page, and without this connection, the elements can appear to be floating. Connections can be achieved by placing each element so that it touches, or even overlaps another one, or by using embellishments such as ribbon or fiber to link items.

Harmony and unity

A harmonious design will present a unifying idea or theme where nothing distracts the viewer from the whole. The best way to check your design for harmony is to step back from it, maybe even hang it up on the wall so that you can see it completely. Now ask yourself, is anything in the design dominant? Do you see a pattern? Is your eye drawn to a focal point? Is anything distracting? Some of the answers to these questions might be exactly what you wanted, while others might surprise you.

The placement of photographs of people can have an effect upon the overall harmony of your page. The eyes of your subjects should look straight at you or toward the center of your album. This helps viewers to stay focused on your design and leads them through the elements on the page. It is often difficult to work out why a design is not working, but taking a step back from your work can help establish whether or not the overall effect is harmonious.

g too far,
Then can
ibly find out
you can go.

There are 3 ways to
get to the top of a
tree:
1. sit on an acorn
2. make friends
   with a bird
3. climb it

Summer

Cropping a picture

1 Place two "L" shaped pieces of card over the photograph and move these around to find the focal point.

2 Once the focus of the picture has been determined, mark the corners lightly with a pencil or acid free pen.

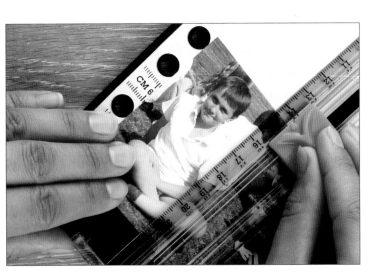

3 Using the pencil marks as a guide, trim around the photograph using a craft knife, or paper trimmer.

4 The finished result is a less cluttered picture that centers upon the focal point – the subject.

Ruth

Designer: Mandy Webb

This layout shows the rule of thirds put into practice (see page 30).

grace was in all her steps.
heaven in her eye.

- John Milton

Visual triangle

Designer: Mandy Webb

This layout is a perfect example of a visual triangle using triadic colors

Eternal Rome

Designer: Karen McIvor

This is a balanced layout – one large image is balanced by a group of smaller ones.

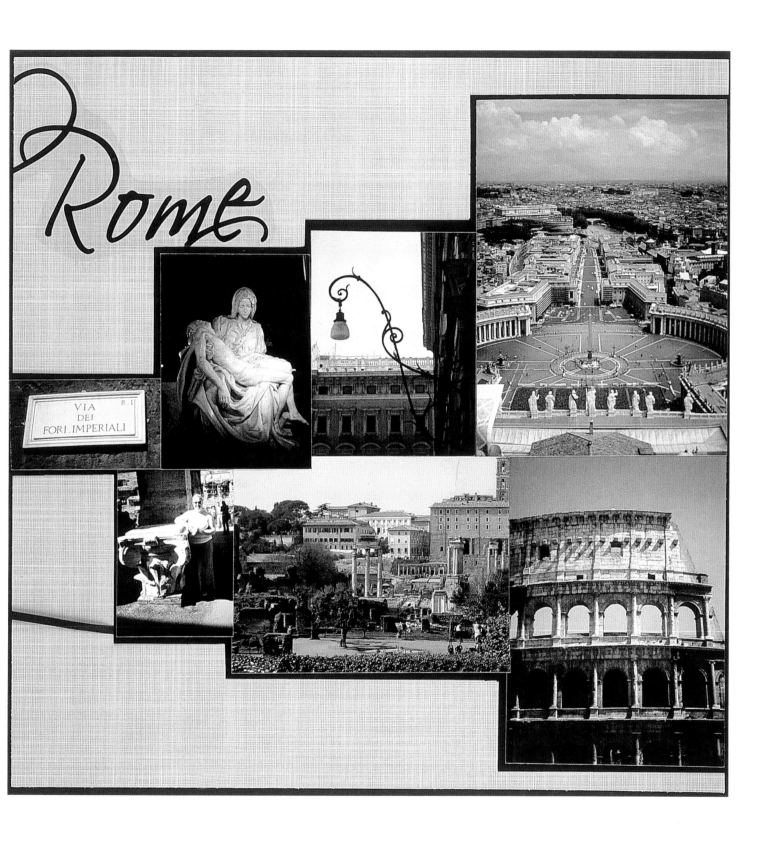

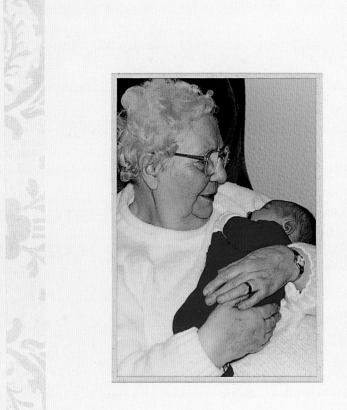

Aching Arm

Designer: Karen McIvor

Pre-cut perspectives allow
you to make quick and
simple symmetrical layouts.

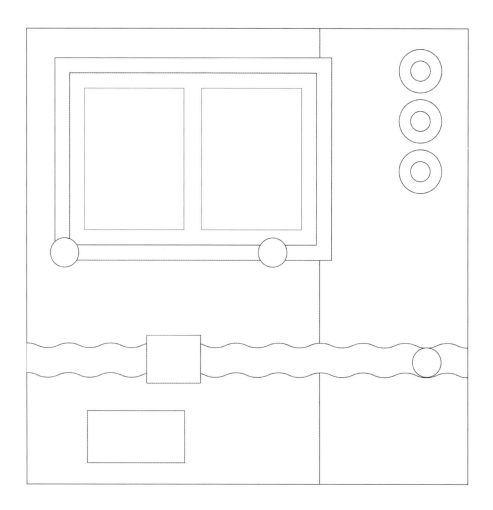

Plan your layouts by making a sketch. One layout sketch can be used for many different pages.

The rule of thirds

Choosing the right place for your design elements will be easier if you use the so-called "rule of thirds." Divide your background into thirds vertically and horizontally, so forming a grid of nine squares. The eye is naturally drawn to the points at which these lines intersect, and these are therefore prime places to locate your focal-point pictures.

If you have only one large portrait-type picture, try to align the eyes of the subject with one of these intersections. If you have multiple images, play around with them, placing them on the intersections of the thirds, and you will see for yourself the difference it makes. The human eye is very sensitive to lines, real or imaginary, and the use of the rule of thirds is a good way to lead the eye to what you want it to see. This principle is used in some of the most beautiful paintings, photographs, and architecture. Start to analyze the proportions of pictures, paintings, and other things you like, and try to establish whether thirds play a part in their composition.

Planning

It may sound obvious, but try planning your design before you start making it. That way you can build in the balance appropriate to the style of photographs you are using and the color of the materials that you have to hand. Use a sheet of squared paper for your plan and mark out an area that corresponds to the scrapbook format you are using. With a pencil, draw in the

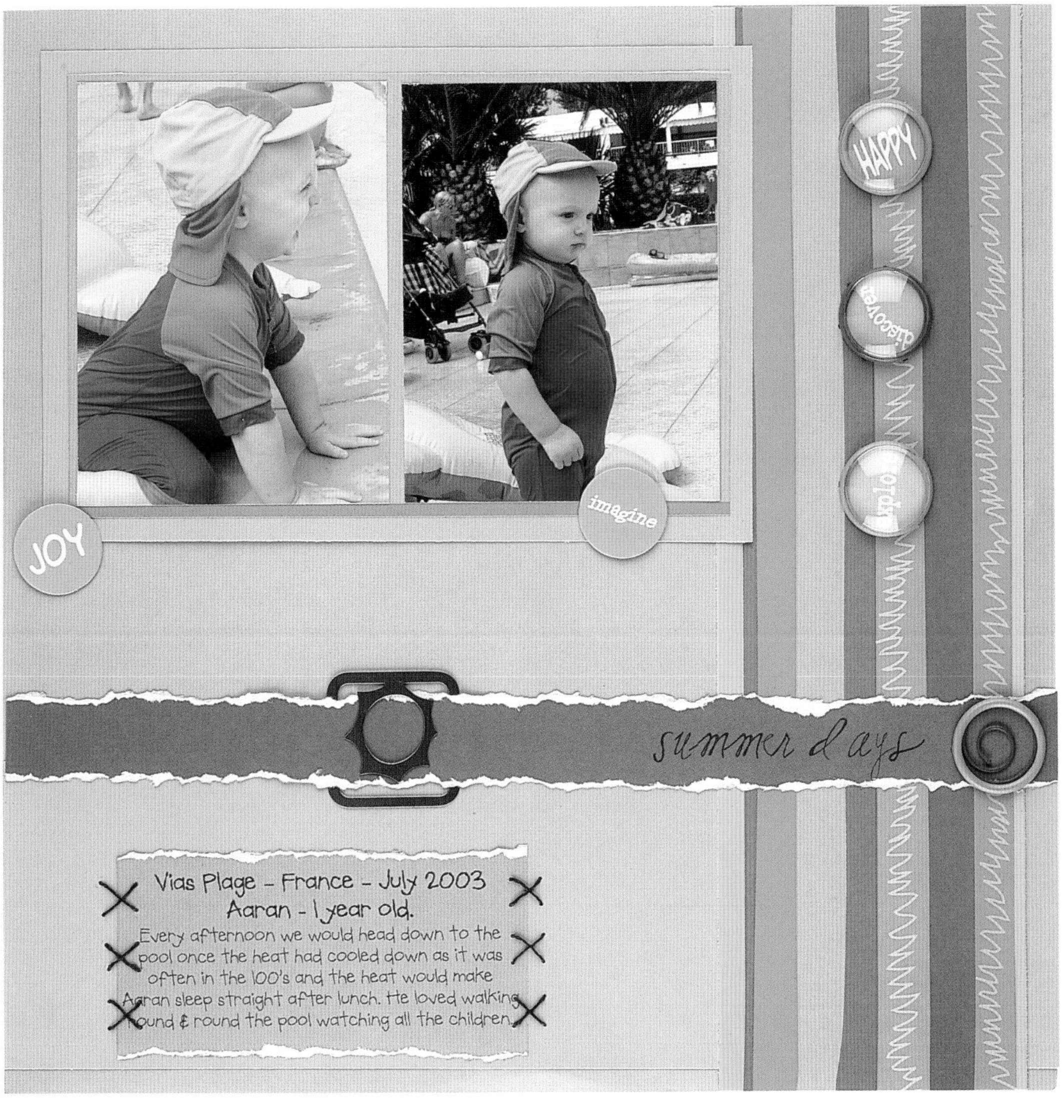
HAPPY
discover
explore
JOY
imagine
summer days
Vias Plage - France - July 2003
Aaran - 1 year old.
Every afternoon we would head down to the pool once the heat had cooled down as it was often in the 100's and the heat would make Aaran sleep straight after lunch. He loved walking round & round the pool watching all the children.

Summer Days

Designer: Sarah Mason

This page was made from a sketch for the composition, but the colors and choice of papers were chosen to match the photographs.

elements you intend to incorporate into your design. Make these as close to scale as possible to get the best representation of the finished design. If the sketch appears balanced, the chances are that the design will work on the page when it is made.

Planning the design can avoid expensive mistakes, and helps you see if your design is balanced, and acheives the effect that you had in mind. The combinations are endless and are a great way to start experimenting with designs, material, and color.

If you find a design that catches your eye, sketch out its key design elements, rather than trying to reproduce the page exactly. This will help you to learn some of the key aspects of composition.

Checklist

The design principles outlined in this chapter will help you create your next scrapbook page. You might think that there is a lot to think about, but it can be simplified into five straightforward questions:

- Does your page have a focal point?
- Is the design symmetrical or asymmetrical and does this match the style of the photos?
- Can you visualize lines at the "thirds" on your page using the rule of thirds?
- Are the elements of your design visually linked?
- Does the page appear as one harmonious design?

Ask yourself these questions as you work on future scrapbook pages, and, before you know it, these principles will be second nature.

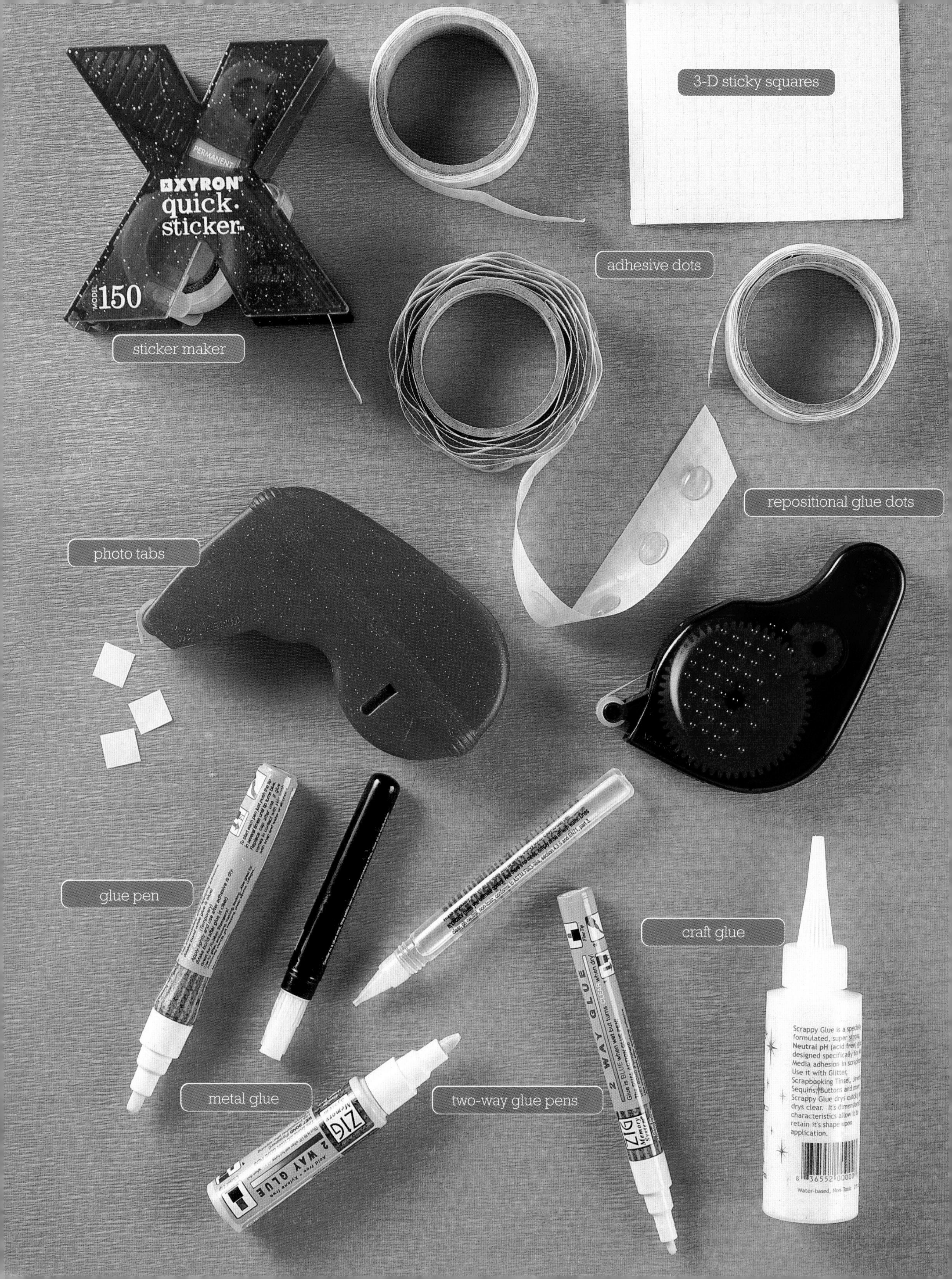

3-D sticky squares

sticker maker

adhesive dots

repositional glue dots

photo tabs

glue pen

craft glue

metal glue

two-way glue pens

Adhesives

It is a good idea to have at least one of each of these types of adhesive in your toolkit, as every one has a unique and special use. Try using your adhesives in creative ways, combining them with other techniques to create scrapbook pages to treasure.

The types of adhesives you select to use in your scrapbook can have a significant impact upon the photographs that are placed within it. Scrapbook adhesives should be pH neutral, acid free, or archival to ensure that your pictures are protected. All scrapbookers have their own preferences in relation to adhesives. Consider trying a broad range of products to find those that work for you. Practice and experimentation will quickly highlight your favorites and their most effective methods of use.

Photo tabs

These are squares of double-sided permanent adhesive tape, available as individual tabs on a roll and also in dispensers. They are ideal for attaching paper and cardstock permanently, and are thin enough to be virtually undetectable. Use photo tabs to attach photographs to mounts before or after trimming and to attach mounts to background cardstock. Photo tabs are usually opaque and are therefore not suitable for attaching sheer or transparent materials such as vellum or acetate.

Repositionable adhesive

This glue is available in a pen dispenser as well as an aerosol, and is perfect for use during the designing process, when elements are being moved around the page. Card and paper can be easily separated after using this glue, and the adhesive can be rubbed off using a finger. The adhesive is applied as tiny dots of dry glue over the surface it is applied to. These tiny dots make it the ideal adhesive for attaching ribbon and fabric.

Repositionable adhesive will also help you use up your scraps of card or paper using your computer (see page 116). Print some text or an image onto regular paper, then attach a scrap of card or paper over the top using repositionable adhesive. Place this back into the printer paper tray and print once again. The text or image will be printed onto the scrap, which can then be easily removed and the adhesive rubbed away. Try using this method to print onto fabric, ribbon, or twill tape to create unique and personal embellishments for your pages.

3-D foam pads

These consist of a strip of foam with permanent adhesive on both the upper and lower faces. They are available in a range of colors, sizes, and thicknesses. These pads can be used to add dimension to your designs by lifting them off the layer to which they are attached. You can also add drama and interest to a focal-point picture by attaching it to the background with 3-D pads. Try using them to lift tags and other embellishments off the page – and out of the ordinary. To make sure that these pads are invisible, attach each one in a position that is slightly inset from the edge of the card or paper. Take care that foam pads are evenly distributed over the reverse of the picture or embellishment to produce a level result. Large areas without pads can "sink," resulting in a concave project.

Using 3-D pads can make your pages slightly bulkier than some other adhesives, and you may need to consider purchasing page protectors that are specifically for dimensional designs.

Adhesive dots

These glue dots can be found in many different sizes, from tiny and ultra thin to large and three dimensional. Adhesive dots are perfect for attaching metal and other heavier embellishments. They are produced on a roll of release paper, which, if unrolled, will reveal a regular line of dots of glue. To use, simply press the item against the dot and peel away the release paper. The glue dot will transfer onto the item and is ready to be attached where required. Glue dots are ideal for items with uneven surfaces; the glue molds itself around the shape, making it simple to attach. The dots of glue can be reduced in

size by trimming them with scissors while still attached to the release paper, although this can be a little awkward and messy. Adhesive dots are available only as circles, and this may not be a suitable or convenient shape for some projects. They can be clear or slightly colored, so for those occasions when it is important that an adhesive is as invisible as possible, be sure to chose a clear version.

Glue sticks

The screw-up sticks of glue used for school projects are safe to use on scrapbook pages. If cost is a concern, it is also worth noting that these sticks, which come in a number of sizes, are some of the cheapest adhesives available. Glue sticks tend to react with paper in the same way as many wet adhesives, causing it to buckle as it dries. For this reason, they are best used on heavier-weight cardstock. Glue sticks can be used to produce a thin, even coverage of adhesive, and are perfect for using when covering journals, tags, and mini-books.

Glue pens

A simple way to carry adhesive around, these are available in a number of different pen widths to enable fine or general application. They contain a wet glue, which initially needs to be drawn down by gently depressing the pen tip a number of times. Some brands contain an adhesive that is permanent when used while wet and repositionable when it is tacky. Printed vellums or transparencies can be attached by careful use of a glue pen. Place tiny dots of adhesive randomly over the back of the sheet, ensuring that each dot is behind a printed letter or image. Wait until the adhesive becomes tacky and then attach the sheet to the background.

Glue pens are ideal for fine or intricate application for use with glitter or sand. Try writing a word or tracing over an image with a glue pen before applying glitter, then shake off the excess to produce a project that will make an impact.

Metal glue

These are specifically formulated for attaching metal embellishments. Metals are often very difficult to attach permanently to paper because their weight contributes to problems with adhesion. Metal glues dry slowly and very hard, making attaching metals and other heavier items simple. They are wet adhesives and are more commonly available in a pen dispenser.

Craft glue

Acid-free craft glue is safe and cheap to use in scrapbooking. Usually water-based PVA, these adhesives tend to be fast and clear drying. They dry to a

Xyron® stickers

1 To use a sticker maker, print or draw your motif onto paper of the correct size and insert in the top of the machine.

2 As you pull the motif out of the other end following the manufacturer's instructions, it should appear with an extra layer on the back, and an acetate film on the right side.

high shine and can be used like a varnish for embellishments on your page. Try coating a tag with a thin layer of craft glue and then applying crumpled tissue paper. The tissue appears to "sink" into the glue and gives a subtle textured surface when dry. Thicker types of craft glue will retain their shape when dry and can be used to add dimension to your pages.

Glazes

These are a formulation of adhesives that dry to a clear, high-shine finish. They are often quite thick, and can be applied in pools or puddles to give the effect of glass, water, or ice. This type of adhesive is ideal for attaching clear or translucent embellishments such as beads, glass, and plastic, because a thin application of the glue is practically invisible. You could try filling the center of a lettered concho with glaze to mimic a typewriter key and create a great embellishment. Also, you could color some glaze with watercolors or dye-based inks to coordinate with the themes of your page: a brown-tinted glaze will give a wonderful sepia tint to anything it is applied to.

Glazes can take a long time to dry – up to 24 hours if applied thickly. Do not be tempted to try to accelerate the process by using a heat gun or hair dryer, as this can result in bubbling or ripples, affecting the final finish.

Sticker maker

Although the other adhesives in this chapter have been referred to generically, the sticker maker system is unique and frequently used by scrapbookers. A Xyron® machine can quickly apply a thin layer of adhesive to one side of any item passed through it. Permanent and repositionable adhesive cartridges are available, and the machines range in size to accommodate items 1½ in. to 9 in. (4 cm to 23 cm) wide. Fabric, ribbon, mesh, or cord can be passed through the machine and will attach instantly to your page. Bulky items cannot be accommodated, but try experimenting with buttons and charms to create fast and effective self-adhesive embellishments.

This is a large size Xyron® sticker maker that will take a letter size sheet.

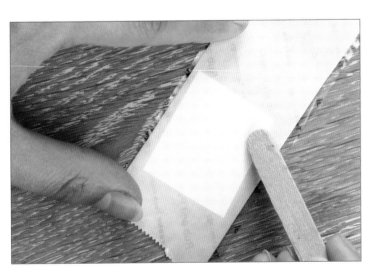

3 Turn to the wrong side, and using a blunt instrument, like a wooden spatula or stick, rub to ensure overall adhesion and to get rid of any air bubbles.

4 Peel off the top coat, and then the backing, and you have your own self adhesive stickers to use on your pages. For larger images use a larger scale machine.

colored papers

printed vellum

printed accent papers

transparency

double-dipped paper

Card, Paper, Vellum, and Transparencies

These four materials form the backbone of all scrapbook pages, onto which can be added all manner of embellishments. How you choose to combine them will depend upon your personal taste and style – the permutations are endless, and that is one of their attractions for many scrapbookers.

Paper

These come in two standard sizes for scrapbooking: 12 in. x 12 in. and 8½ in. x 11½ in. (30 cm x 30 cm and 21 cm x 28 cm). One of the first purchases made by scrapbookers is a pile of patterned scrapbook papers. The range of patterns can be overwhelming, and it is often difficult to know where to start. Paper is usually single sided and sheets are available flat (smooth), embossed, and glittered. Patterns range from cute to sophisticated, and even include photo-real images such as grass, wood, and pebbles.

It can be easier to match your photographs to the paper than vice versa, so consider taking a selection of pictures with you to the scrapbook store. Look at the background of the picture: is there something that you can highlight with a patterned or plain paper? Look at the clothes that the subjects of your photograph are wearing: can you use a complementary texture or color? There are so many papers to choose from that you are bound to find something that will bring out the very best in your photographs.

Cardstock

This tends to be thicker than paper and therefore makes a good background or base for any design. Plain cardstock is available in a huge range of colors that is sure to meet the needs of any scrapbooker. Although plain-colored cardstock may appear less exciting than patterned, this can be a good first purchase, as most pages rely on some element of plain card in the design. Also, plain colors can be easier to start with, and practicing some of the principles of composition can be simpler with plain card, as there is less to distract the eye. It is a good idea to purchase three sheets at a time of the same color, as this allows one sheet for each page of a double layout and a spare sheet for accents, embellishments, or errors. It can be so frustrating to make a mistake and have to redesign your page or make another trip to the store.

Tearing card and paper

Look carefully at the paper and cardstock you purchase: some sheets will be a single color throughout the whole thickness, while others will have a white core. This can have an impact upon the finished result when you cut or tear an edge. Card and paper can be torn to size to produce a finish that has additional interest and texture. Tearing reveals their layers, and card or paper with a white core will produce layers of white to contrast with the color of the finished surface. (Note that the torn edges of single-colored card can be chalked or inked to produce this contrast.)

You can tear card or paper with a white core in two different ways: to produce a layered tear, which reveals the core, or to create a tear that leaves the core hidden. To produce a layered tear, start by holding the card with one hand and begin to tear toward you from the top edge with the other hand. To tear the left edge of the card, tear toward you with the left hand; for the right edge tear with the right hand. Move slowly down the length of the card to control the direction of the tear.

To produce a torn edge that does not reveal the core of the card, simply tear away from you. This gives a sharper edge with no transition from the finished layer of the card.

Acid-free

Scrapbook card and papers should be acid free to ensure that your photographs and scrapbooks last as long as possible. Acid is used in the manufacturing process of paper to break down the wood pulp fibers and produce a high-quality, smooth paper. However, any residual acid in scrapbook paper can react with your photographs and cause them to fade and yellow, accelerating their deterioration.

Acid-free card and paper has been processed to remove any residual acid, usually by the addition of calcium carbonate. This process is usually referred

to as "buffering." Acid-free card and paper will have a pH of 7 (neutral) or higher. Some good-quality paper for photocopying or printing is acid free – it can be surprising what is safe to use in your album.

The only way to be sure that what you are using is safe is to test it with the pH-testing kits and pens that are now available. A section of the paper is treated with the test and produces a color change that indicates the relative pH value of the product. The results are reliable for light to mid-toned paper but ineffective for dark colors as the color change cannot be seen.

Try making your own paper, adding calcium carbonate to buffer any acid that might remain in the pulp. You can produce some beautiful papers to embellish your work and can be sure that they are safe to use.

Lignin-free paper

A naturally occurring substance found in wood, "lignin" is one of the most abundant substances on earth. Together with cellulose, lignin forms one of the main components of woody tissue. This bonding element is separated from wood by the chemical pulping processes employed to produce paper.

Lignin causes paper to change color and become brittle over time, which can have a significant impact on the lifespan of your scrapbook. It can be removed during the paper-making process, but these additional steps incur extra cost, which is one of the reasons why scrapbook cardstock and paper can be slightly more expensive than other craft papers.

One of the worst papers for acid and lignin content is newsprint – in only a few months the pages begin to yellow and become brittle. This is worth remembering if newspaper clippings form part of your memorabilia for a page. Acid-neutralizing archive sprays can be used to treat paper-based memorabilia such as tickets, greetings cards, and news cuttings to prolong their lifespan. Alternatively, memorabilia could be placed in pockets or envelopes that can be purchased or handmade specifically for this purpose.

There are no rules to say that your album must be acid and lignin free, but it is usually a sensible decision, bearing in mind the possible results.

Vellum

Before paper was first introduced, books were written on parchment and vellum. Vellum was prepared from calfskin, and its smooth, flawless finish was highly prized and very expensive. Modern vellums are highly versatile materials that share the translucent qualities of their medieval counterparts, but are produced as specialty papers. They are sheer or transparent and will allow anything underneath to show through. This unfortunately includes adhesives. There are no glues that are invisible when used with vellum, and therefore scrapbookers have become more inventive in finding methods of attachment, as highlighted in Chapter 4.

Vellums are available in clear, colored, printed, patterned, and plain finishes, together with some that complement designs in manufacturers' ranges. If you cannot find decorated vellum to suit your needs, consider printing your own using your computer, or stamping a design by hand. Words and phrases make great titles, and vellum can also be used for journaling. Change the color of vellum using chalks and pastels to customize colors to suit any page layout.

These papers are not as porous as other cards and paper, and therefore inks and adhesives can take longer to dry. This characteristic can be exploited to produce embossed text or images. Immediately after stamping or printing onto vellum, shake on an embossing powder, then shake off the excess before setting the powder using a heat gun.

In addition to being translucent, these papers are quite delicate. Creases and wrinkles will be more visible than with other paper types, and so care should be taken during handling.

Use vellums to tone down brightly colored backgrounds and produce a soft, muted effect. Also, try using them as mounts and frames for photographs. An ingenious use of vellum is to place a plain piece over an out-of-focus photograph. As if by magic, the picture appears to come back into focus, and so an otherwise useless image can be incorporated in your scrapbook.

Like other papers and cardstock, vellums can be torn and layered. This can produce a gorgeous graduation of color quickly and simply. If you are familiar with

our FAMILY

The LOVE in

photo-editing software, try adjusting a photograph negative to 50 percent and then printing this on vellum. It produces the most fabulously soft images that are just perfect for pictures of babies and children.

Transparencies

The crystal-clear quality of a transparency will allow the full depth of the color of your background to show through. This can be important when you do not want the softer muting achieved with vellum.

Transparencies, or acetate sheets, are commercially available in 12 in. x 12 in. (30 cm x 30 cm) size and can be used as they are or trimmed to completely cover smaller formats. Many of these products are pre-printed with text and/or images, providing a dramatic impact when placed over your work.

The key thing to consider when using transparencies is that they work better when incorporated in layers.

Add ribbon or even dried flowers to the background before laying over the transparency, and suddenly the whole layout begins to hang together. Arrange text so that it runs over some or all of a photograph to really draw the eye into the design.

Make your own transparencies using an ink jet printer. As long as the transparency is PVC- and acid-free it will be safe to incorporate into your album. Print journaling onto a transparency and layer it over a photograph or tag for a twist on the usual form of telling your story. How about stamping text or an image onto a transparency to make a great embellishment? Create unusual photographic images by printing directly onto a transparency. The result will be softer than when using photographic paper and can be layered over a regular print of the same size to give a feeling of depth and vibrant color.

The Love in our Family

Designer: Alison Docherty

Layers of cardstock and patterned papers give this page a distinctive look.

fancy brads

mini eyelets

eyelet template

eyelets

Eyelet Friend ™
Eyelet Placement Templat
For 1/8" Eyelets
www.timelesstouches.net

1/2"
1"
1 1/2"
2"
3/4"
1 1/4"
1 3/4"
2 1/4"

shaped clips

decorative eyelet

seasonal brads

setting mat

conchos

nailheads

snaps

Fasteners

Whether you use fasteners for practical, decorative purposes, or both, they are a simple way to hold the layers of your page together. Look for fasteners in your stationery store as well as craft suppliers – there is a host of products that could be incorporated into your designs. Paperclips and mini bulldog clips can attach card- and paper-based design elements in a formal or relaxed way. These are available in a range of sizes and colors that are sure to complement most themes.

There are five types of basic fasteners used in scrapbooking: eyelets, snaps, nailheads, conchos, and brads. Each of these can be used as an alternative to glue to attach card, paper, vellums, fibers, transparencies, and fabric. They come in a variety of shapes, sizes, and colors, and can often add just the right touch to enhance your scrapbook layouts. Other fasteners, which do not pierce the page and do not need any special equipment to attach them, such as clips and buckles, are also widely available.

Eyelets

These come in a wide variety of themes, shapes, sizes, and colors, and the overwhelming choice can sometimes make it difficult to decide which to use. The standard eyelet sizes are $\frac{1}{16}$ in., $\frac{1}{8}$ in., and $\frac{3}{16}$ in. (2 mm, 4 mm, and 6 mm), and most are made from non-corroding metals. Eyelets have a circular hole in the center that forms a post protruding from the back of the eyelet.

Setting an eyelet requires specialty tools that form part of the basic essential tool kit. A hammer, punch, setter, and setting mat make up the eyelet toolkit, with different punches used to make holes for each of the three basic eyelet sizes. A universal setter will set any size of eyelet, although individual setter heads are available for each size. (As well as being used for eyelets and snaps, these tools can be used to produce punched holes in a range of sizes for lacing or stitching card and paper.) To set an eyelet into a piece of cardstock, work on a firm, stable surface such as a kitchen worktop or hard floor (a table that has any "give" or spring will make the job harder). Place the setting mat on the surface and put your card on top. Select the correct size of punch for the eyelet being used and place it on the card where required. Use the hammer to tap the top of the punch firmly two or three times to create the hole. Pass an eyelet through the hole and turn the card over (the post of the eyelet will be protruding from the back of the card). Place the setting tool in the center of the eyelet post and tap the setter firmly three times. This will split the post and roll it flat on the surface of the card, so setting the eyelet. Make more holes and insert eyelets as necessary. There are now products available that help with the even spacing of eyelets, or you could just use a ruler and pencil.

Snaps

These fasteners are similar to eyelets in that they require the eyelet tool kit to attach them to your page. They do not have the central hole of an eyelet, and give the appearance of a small button or nailhead.

Snaps are attached in the same way as eyelets, with a hole of the correct size punched initially and the post set on the reverse. Ensure that you do not hammer too hard when setting a snap, as the front can easily be distorted. Tap the setter firmly once, then check the front of the snap before tapping again.

SNAP IDEAS

• Use snaps to attach the layers of your page as well as decorative elements.

• Use three snaps in a row to attach a journaling box – not at the top but down one side. This will intrigue the eye and add interest.

• Use a snap as a hanger for a frame or mounted photograph.

• Use decorative snaps that resemble screw heads and bolts for fun accents that can be used to complement a suitable theme.

EYELET
IDEAS

• Thread fibers through an eyelet in the top of a tag.

• Attach vellum by setting an eyelet in each corner.

• A line of eyelets can be a feature on its own.

•Try using eyelets to create the spine of a mini-book by folding two pieces of card in half and sliding them together to make a four-page card. Score a narrow spine near the folded edge of all four leaves of the book before setting eyelets in the gap between the fold and the scored line.

• Hang tags and other embellishments from ribbon threaded through eyelets set in the background cardstock.

• Lacing ribbon crisscross fashion through parallel lines of eyelets creates a simple border detail.

Brads

Available in a wide range of shapes, sizes, and colors, brads (also known as paper fasteners) have a solid domed top that will show on the right side of the project and two flat prongs protruding from the back.

To attach a brad, start by making a hole in your project with a piercing tool. This will make attaching the brad easier and will prevent damage to both the cardstock and the prongs. Push the prongs of the brad through the card from the right side. Turn your project over and pull the brad gently to ensure it is completely through the card. Separate the two prongs at the back of the brad and bend them back until they are flat to the reverse surface of the card.

The prongs of some brads can be very long and these can sometimes show on the right side of a project when attached. Try rotating the brad a little, and the prongs will move around. If this does not solve the problem, cut off the protruding section of the prongs with a sturdy pair of scissors.

Use brads to reinforce other adhesives in areas subject to high stresses. The top edges of a page protector can easily become damaged, so try attaching a brad at these points to provide additional support.

Fasten bundles of tags or mounted photographs together by punching a hole at the top or in a corner and then passing a brad through. The individual pages will be able to move freely on the brad to create a tag book. A small book can be made by attaching several layers together (see below) as in the steps for making a swingbook on page 106.

Attach two brads side by side before winding thin ribbon in a figure of eight around them both. Try using this method to fasten the flap of an envelope or gatefold doors on a small book.

Fixing an eyelet

1 Using an eyelet hole punch and small hammer, punch out the appropriate sized hole for your eyelet.

2 Place the eyelet in the hole on the right side of your work.

3 Holding the eyelet carefully, turn the paper over so that the tube is showing.

4 Using an eyelet setter and small hammer, set the eyelet by giving it a short tap on the reverse.

Right: A concho acts as the perfect frame for letters or whole words.

Conchos

The concho is attached through the background cardstock with prongs in exactly the same way as a nailhead, but instead of being solid they form a frame. Look for conchos in a range of sizes to make titles or add to journaling.

Add decorative elements such as lettering to the center before fixing the concho in place. Conchos containing lettering can be arranged in a line to reproduce the effect of typewriter keys.

Fill the center with a glaze adhesive after fixing to create an even more convincing effect.

Use conchos to highlight a word or phrase in your journaling (see examples below).

Place a scrap of patterned paper in the center to produce a decorative element.

Try experimenting with different colored embossing powders, permanent markers, or nail polish to create custom-colored conchos, rather than purchasing a number of different colors or finishes.

Nailheads

These are round-topped fasteners with four to five sharp prongs on the underside. They are very easy to use and require no special equipment to attach to your layout. The prongs are simply pushed through the background and fixed on the reverse.

Place your cardstock on a firm surface, with a soft spongy nailhead mat or other padding, such as bubble wrap, a mouse mat, or some corrugated cardboard, between the card and the surface. This will allow the sharp prongs to push through the cardstock without damaging the prongs or the underlying surface. It will also mean that you do not have to push hard to get the prongs through, which can buckle and crease the card. With the padding in position, place the nailhead on the card where required. Use your thumb to apply firm pressure to the nailhead and push the prongs through the card. Turn the project over to reveal the prongs on the reverse side. Place the card back on the firm surface and use a small hammer or the side of a pair of scissors to push the prongs over and flatten them until they are level with the surface of the reverse of the card

Fixing a concho

1 Using a soft surface, or a setting mat, to protect the table, position your concho or nailhead on your page.

2 With your fingers, push the sharp points through the cardstock.

3 With the back of an old spoon, or other blunt instrument, fold over the sharp points on the reverse side.

Make as many conchos as you like to add detail and decoration to your page.

tonal color wheel

rainbow color selector

basic color wheels

primary mixing wheel

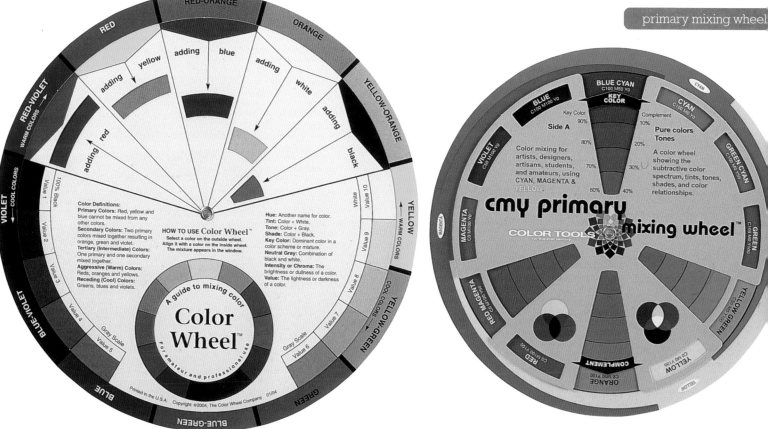

PICK, POINT AND MATCH®

RAINBOW®
COLOR SELECTOR

The handy tool for perfect color
combinations every time.

Escoja, Apunte y Emparaje™
El instrumento útil para las combinaciones
de colores siempre perfectas.

Choisissez, Identifiez et Agencez™
A utiliser avec les tissus, fibres, arrangements
floraux, papiers ou peintures.

Basic Color Wheel

RED-ORANGE
RED
ORANGE
RED-VIOLET
YELLOW-ORANGE
WARM COLORS
adding yellow
adding blue
adding white
adding red
adding black
VIOLET
COOL COLORS
YELLOW
WARM COLORS
100% Black
Value 1
Value 2
Value 3
Value 4
Value 5
Gray Scale
BLUE-VIOLET
White
Value 10
Value 9
Value 8
Value 7
Value 6
Gray Scale
COOL COLORS
YELLOW-GREEN
BLUE
GREEN
BLUE-GREEN

Color Definitions:
Primary Colors: Red, yellow and blue cannot be mixed from any other colors.
Secondary Colors: Two primary colors mixed together resulting in orange, green and violet.
Tertiary (Intermediate) Colors: One primary and one secondary mixed together.
Aggressive (Warm) Colors: Reds, oranges and yellows.
Receding (Cool) Colors: Greens, blues and violets.

HOW TO USE Color Wheel
Select a color on the outside wheel.
Align it with a color on the inside wheel.
The mixture appears in the window.

Hue: Another name for color.
Tint: Color + White.
Tone: Color + Gray.
Shade: Color + Black.
Key Color: Dominant color in a color scheme or mixture.
Neutral Gray: Combination of black and white.
Intensity or Chroma: The brightness or dullness of a color.
Value: The lightness or darkness of a color.

A guide to mixing color
Color Wheel™
For amateur and professional use

Printed in the U.S.A. Copyright ©2004, The Color Wheel Company 01/04

CMY Primary Mixing Wheel

BLUE CYAN
C100 M50 Y0
KEY COLOR
BLUE
C100 M100 Y0
CYAN
Key Color C100 M0 Y0
Side A
90%
Complement
10%
Pure colors
Tones
VIOLET
C50 M100 Y0
80%
20%
Color mixing for artists, designers, artisans, students, and amateurs, using CYAN, MAGENTA & YELLOW.
70%
30%
A color wheel showing the subtractive color spectrum, tints, tones, shades, and color relationships.
GREEN CYAN
MAGENTA
C0 M100 Y0
60%
40%
50%
GREEN
C100 M0 Y100
cmy primary
mixing wheel™
COLOR TOOLS
for the 21st century
RED MAGENTA
YELLOW GREEN
RED
ORANGE
COMPLEMENT
YELLOW
C0 M0 Y100

In the same way that the colors we choose to wear can affect the way we feel, the colors we use with our photographs can affect the emotional impact of our pictures. Look around you at stores and magazines, and you will be bombarded with color combinations all designed to have different effects.

In this chapter we will look in depth at the color wheel and how to combine colors to produce pages that bring out the best in your photographs. A basic knowledge of color theory can help when selecting schemes for your pages. Understanding how colors relate to each other can be useful when faced with a picture that is difficult to scrapbook, and can help to produce a layout with maximum impact.

The color wheel

Colors are divided into primary, secondary, and tertiary colors. Red, yellow, and blue are the primaries, which cannot be created by combining any other color. Mixing any two of these colors together creates the secondary colors of orange, green, and violet. By mixing a primary color with its adjacent secondary color, the tertiary colors of red/orange, red/violet, yellow/green, yellow/orange, blue/green, and blue/violet can be created. All twelve primary, secondary, and tertiary colors are included in the color wheel like sections on a clock. If the primary colors were located at 12, 4, and 8 o'clock, the secondary colors would be at 2, 6, and 10, with the tertiary colors filling the remaining spaces.

Try to think of the color wheel as a map to help you locate colors, enabling you to visualize how they relate

to each other. Although you can create a color wheel for yourself quite simply, commercial color wheels are available that include tints and shades. These can produce endless options for color schemes and combinations. Do not be put off by the apparent complexity of some color wheels – the basic information is very much the same.

This commercial color wheel shows tints, tones, and shades. Colors are exposed in the windows as the top wheel is moved around.

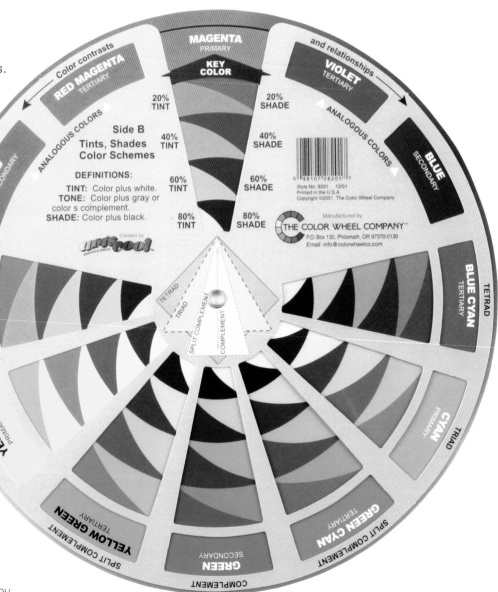

Mixing colors

The 12 colors on the color wheel can be added to by mixing them with white or black, or with each other. Adding white to a color lightens it and creates a tint: for example, pink is a tint of red. Adding black deepens a color and makes a darker shade, e.g. burgundy. Further mixing of colors can create myriad shades, tints, and hues.

Warm and cool colors

Colors can evoke feelings and emotions in much the same way as music. Much of this feeling is created by the "temperature value" of each color. Most colors can be separated into either warm or cool colors. Examples of basic warm and cool colors are:

Warm	Cool
Red	Blue
Orange	Green
Yellow	Violet

The tertiary colors would generally take the temperature value of the dominant primary, e.g. yellow/green would be a warm color because of its yellow content. Working with the temperature value of a color can produce a co-ordinated pallete that provides a great deal of energy on the page. Think about matching color temperature with the seasons of the year, for example, to create fresh, cool spring pages or vibrant and warm fall projects.

Mixing cool and warm colors can also add to your pages. Try adding a dash of a warm color to a predominantly cool page, and suddenly the page seems to have a little excitement. Our eyes are drawn to contrasts, and this can be used to produce great effects with warm and cool colors.

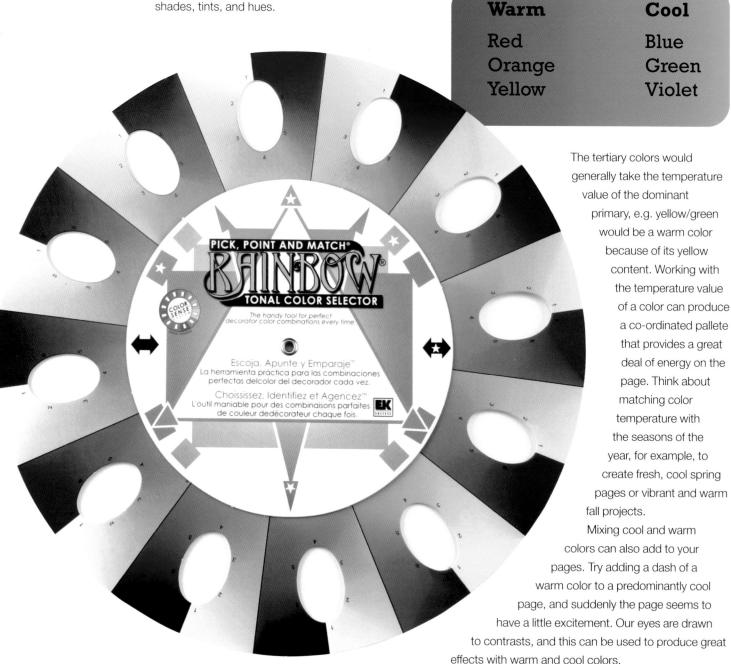

Monochromatic schemes

One of the simplest ways to use the color wheel is to look at a single color. Working with shades and tints of the same color will produce a monochromatic scheme that will always work well. These color schemes are safe and easy on the eye. Some manufacturers produce packs of cardstock in monochromatic colors, making it simple to find shades and tints. However, it can be fun to find an unusual color in a photograph and then build on this to create a monochromatic palette.

Complementary colors

Colors that are directly opposite each other on the color wheel are known as "complementary." When these colors are used together, they seem to make each

other brighter and more intense.

Complementary schemes produce the most extreme contrasts and produce a visual energy that captures the eye. This does not mean that complementary colors are necessarily bright – soft pink and pale green placed together can create the same visual impact as deep red and bottle green – because the energy is created by the combination of these colors, not the colors themselves.

A dash of a complementary color on your scrapbook page adds a little visual excitement. It can be surprising what a difference these combinations can make. Combine a shade, tint or tone of the color directly opposite the base color on the color wheel, and observe the effect.

A Godson

Designer: Karen McIvor

A good example of a monochromatic scheme.

Triadic schemes

Selecting three evenly spaced colors on the wheel produces a triadic scheme. These colors could just be the primaries, or they could be more unusual combinations such as eggplant, sage, and orange, or lime, peach, and cornflower. Consider matching one color from your photographs and finding the triadic colors that complement it.

Using equal proportions of color on your scrapbook page can result in projects that present a great deal of information for the eyes to process, which can prove tiring. Although this can apply to any color scheme, it is a particular consideration for triadic color combinations.

One way to address this can be to use the colors in unequal amounts. Allow one color to dominate, perhaps as the background for the design, and this will produce a visual flow across the whole page. Then use about half this amount for the second color – perhaps for

photo mounts, tags, or journaling boxes. Finally, use the third color in a very small quantity to provide visual punch, as an accent for embellishments for example. This ratio is also known as "Quart, pint, ounce," where the quart represents the largest amount of color and the ounce the smallest. This is an easily remembered ratio that can make all the difference to the harmony of your work.

Analogous colors

Neighboring, or analogous colors on the wheel are related, making them harmonious in combination. By selecting a single color on the wheel and the colors immediately on each side, you can create a three-color scheme that blends and tones.

If you are feeling more adventurous, use the colors on either side of your threesome to provide you with five linked colors to experiment with. This also allows you to use the differing shades or tones of the same colors.

Born

MAY 1927

Putham

pears competition winners
official photograph

Spent much of their infancy
in separate orphanages

Evacuated and forced to spend many of
their childhood years in children's homes

Leonard and Joan Speechley

torn apart by circumstances

46   A Genealogical History

THUS end...
...and F...

T O R N

Tetrads

Color schemes combining four hues, known as tetrads, produce bold or sophisticated combinations. Placing a square over the center of your color wheel will show you options for combining four equally spaced colors. Move the square around to indicate more options until you find one that you like. By replacing the square with a rectangle, a new set of combinations of four colors become possible. Consider the visual impact of so much color on a page and bear in mind the impact that the "quart, pint, ounce" proportions can create.

Neutral colors

White, gray, and beige can be found in the center of the color wheel. These colors can be used together to create designs that are timeless and serene. They can be warm or cold, depending on the colors they are created from. There is a "homey" quality to neutrals that makes them comfortable to design with. Neutrals can work particularly well with black-and-white or sepia-toned photographs.

Look at the range of heritage-style cardstock and paper available at your scrapbook store and you will find that neutrals feature significantly. These colors never seem to go out of style – they can be classy and sophisticated or earthy and light. So the next time you are faced with a challenging photograph to scrapbook, look to the neutral palette, as the solution could be right there. The numerous ways in which neutrals can be combined both with themselves and with other colors should make them a staple of any supply of cardstock or paper.

Remember

Designer: Dawn Inskip

A neutral color scheme allows your photograph to be the focus of your layout.

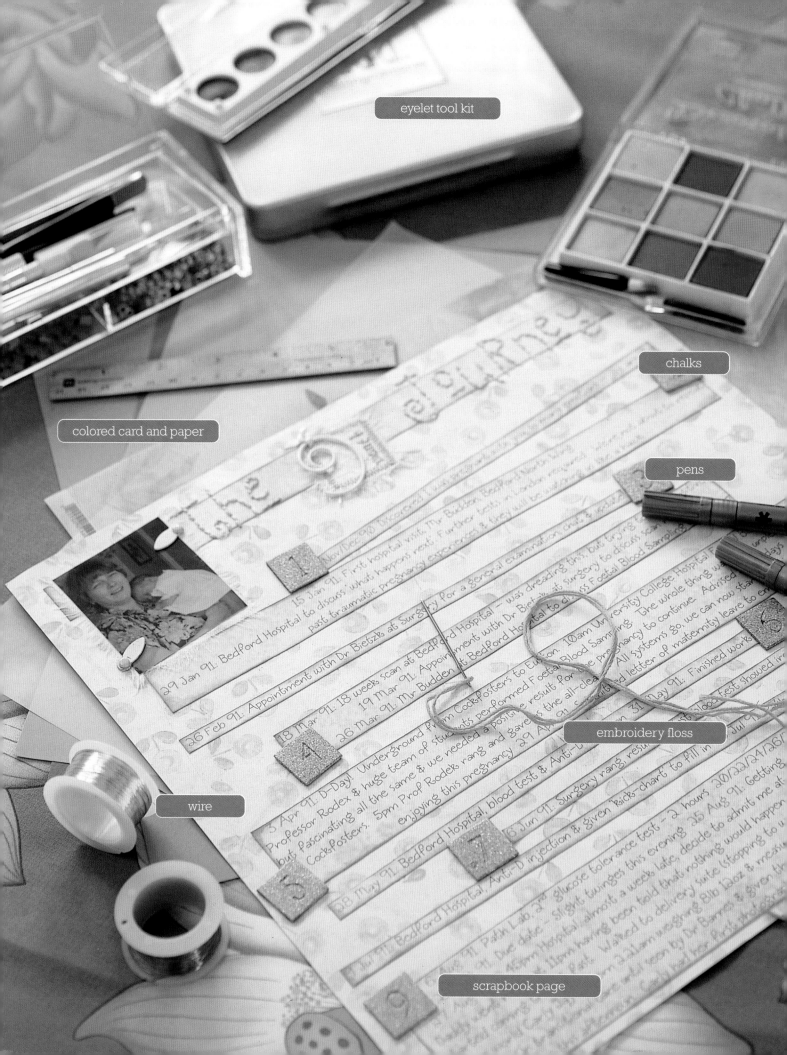

eyelet tool kit

chalks

colored card and paper

pens

embroidery floss

wire

scrapbook page

A scrapbook without journaling can be like a painting without a frame: lovely but not quite finished. Journaling can easily be overlooked both at the design stage and when you are focussing on the techniques you will use to create your projects. But a scrapbook without the stories will be meaningless to future generations.

In this section, you will find ideas and inspiration to help you create journaling for even the most difficult stories. Overcome writer's block by trying out one of these techniques and make your scrapbooking meaningful. If journaling comes easily to you, you might even find a new twist you can incorporate into your stories, so that your words will be treasured by generations to come.

Questions, questions

How many old photograph albums have you looked through and asked, "Who is that?" "Where was this taken?" or "Why were you wearing those?!". If you were fortunate, the person who could answer those questions was at hand and you would have the opportunity to hear the narrative behind the pictures.

If you find it difficult to start journaling, it might help to pretend that you are answering questions. Imagine that, years from now, one of your grandchildren asks you "What were you like when you were little?" These are the stories that are treasured within a family, and can be easily lost if they are not recorded.

Consider turning a topic into a question, and then try to answer as fully as you can. Imagine all the questions that could be asked about the photographs you are including on the page, and try to include as much detail as possible – the classic questions are who, what, where, why and when. The questions can even be incorporated into the journaling in a question-and-answer format to create a fast and simple method of recording the story behind the pictures. Alternatively, record a dialogue using the actual words spoken by some, or all of the subjects within the photograph.

Sheer poetry

If you are looking for a different approach to journaling, then you might like to consider trying a poem. Writing your own piece of poetry brings another personal and creative element to your work. If this is daunting, then there are numerous resources available for poetry and quotations. You could try your local library for books of poetry by your favorite authors: a poem that means something to you will add so much to your scrapbook. Greetings cards often include moving or meaningful poetry, with the additional bonus of being ready-matched for particular occasions and celebrations.

Searching the Internet will produce a host of websites that include resources of poetry, quotations, and page title ideas. These can be searched to produce poetry for a particular theme or to include certain words. There are so many sites that you are certain to find the perfect poem that sums up

Poetry

Designer: Sarah Mason.

If you find writing poetry difficult, then call upon a talented friend who has a way with words. This poem is by Tracy Ogles.

Define It

Designer: Sarah Mason

Ready made definitions are a quick and easy way to add your feelings onto the page.

everything you could wish to say. Keeping a notebook and pen readily to hand can be extremely useful when searching for poetry and quotations for your scrapbook. Use these to make a note of anything that you like, even if you decide not to use it. These notes are sure to come in useful for another project at some later date.

Reportage

If you are afraid that you will miss some important facts when you are journaling your memories, then it might help to take a more journalistic approach to recording the important details. Try following the basic tenets of journalism, asking Who? What? Where? When? Why? and How? This method focusses on gathering the facts and figures relevant to the photographs and can help to keep your journaling to the point. Try selecting just one of these words as the start of an open question, then try

to answer it as fully as possible. This can produce very detailed and sometimes deep journaling that goes beyond what can be seen in the picture.

Get lyrical

A song can have the power to evoke a person, a place, or even a time. A quick look through a music collection can bring back so many memories, so why not link the memories and the music together? Songs can conjure up warm summer evenings, weddings, bedtimes, and many more occasions in our lives. Using song lyrics can be a great way to journal, as the words can often have the same power as the music.

Once you have a song in mind for a scrapbook page, you can source the lyrics from a number of places. If they are not printed inside the record sleeve, cassette box, or CD case, then try searching the Internet, even if you do

not know the title or even the singer(s) in question. If you do not have access to the Internet, enquire at your local library, as they often have access to a host of resources they can search on your behalf.

Define it

A single word can often sum up everything about the photographs on your page. When you have the right word for your project, try looking up its meaning in a dictionary. Definitions have become an increasingly popular way to journal, as they can offer a number of different approaches to the same word. If the dictionary does not inspire you, then you could always try making up your own definitions for your words. This can be as fun or as meaningful as you choose, and that is part of the pleasure of journaling.

A number of manufacturers produce ready-made embellishments based upon definitions. Products include stickers, printed vellums, and labels, and are simple to use. Many of these are available in a range of themes to suit most pages and offer something for everyone.

Word games

Mnemonics are generally used as an aid to memory, but you can use them as a way to gather a relatively large amount of journaling into a small space. Start by selecting a word that will have meaning for the page – this could be a name, a place, or an emotion, for example. Write each letter of the word on a separate line and then try to write a single line about your photographs beginning with each of the letters. Changing the style, color, or size of the text used will help to prevent this from becoming a mass of unreadable words.

Cheeky Boy

Designer: Karen McIvor

A folded cardboard hinge provides the perfect hidden journalling space.

If you want to include a number of words, you could try linking them together like a crossword puzzle. This style of journaling can be visually interesting and form part of the overall design of the project. This theme can be exploited to its fullest extent by using letter tiles from word games. Old games can be found at boot sales and junk shops for very little money, and can add a twist to your journaling. Replica letter tiles are available specifically for scrapbooks, if archival quality is a concern. These combine the memories of childhood days with products that are safe to use with your photographs.

Hidden away

Some journaling can be too sensitive or poignant to read each time you open your scrapbook. This does not mean that these memories should not be included in your pages – after all they are a part of your story, and future generations would get a very distorted view of your life if the only memories recorded were happy ones.

Hidden journaling is one method of including your thoughts, feelings, and memories in your project while preserving a degree of privacy. There are numerous ways to hide journaling, and the more ingenious you are, the more exciting these finds will be in the future.

Try using hinges on a photo mount to produce a space hidden under a photograph. Journaling can be placed underneath and remain inconspicuous. A tag containing journaling can be slipped behind a photo or other design element on the page to create a secret hiding place. Another way to incorporate hidden journaling can be to write a note or letter and place this in a sealed envelope on the page. Envelopes made from patterned paper can become decorative elements in themselves.

Try journaling on a strip of card or paper before folding it concertina-style. This can be tied closed or secured with brads to keep the contents private. Creating a mini-journal or tag book can provide more journaling space if there is a lot to record. Tie a number of pages or tags together after the journaling is complete and wrap it with ribbon or fiber to close. These small projects can be incorporated as elements of the design.

List it

Lists are a quick and simple way to record details, thoughts, and feelings. Free from the restrictions of producing a grammatically correct sentence, this style of journaling can help when faced with writer's block. Try looking at the photographs for your scrapbook page and write down your thoughts as they come into your head. Written in the form of a list, this journaling is short, sharp, and to the point.

Say it your way

Home computers can help to make journaling for your scrapbook a simple task. Spelling- and grammar-checking tools can correct text as it is typed, and a multitude of fonts means that you need never use the same style twice. PCs also allow the possibility of varying the size and color of text to match the theme, mood, or color scheme of your page. It can be very liberating to have the capability to produce such a range of styles of journaling so that the only thing to focus upon is the content. It can, however, be easy to get carried away with fancy fonts, and you may choose one that proves difficult to read. Journaling fonts that resemble handwriting are good choices for simplicity and clarity.

Your handwriting is an important heirloom in its own right. It can be so special to discover handwritten notes on the back of photographs or old letters written by close relatives. Even if you dislike your own handwriting, you should try to make a point of including it at least once in a scrapbook layout to create a record of it.

Handwriting can reveal a great deal about a person and their background. Do you still have traces of copybook lettering in your style? Handwriting is no longer taught in many schools, and so our handwriting may be very different to that of our children. Use pens that are labelled as "archival quality" and "lightfast," as these will resist fading and will be safe to use with your precious photographs.

Break out of your comfort zone and try a different way of producing your journaling. Try to go beyond the ordinary and create something that is more than a

Aaran

Say it Your Way

Designer: Sarah Mason

It is important to include your
handwriting on your layouts,
as future generations will be
left with your personal touch.

collection of photographs arranged in an artistic way. An album will have much more impact in the future if your journaling is meaningful.

You can take your journaling to another level by writing about feelings. Dates, places, and times can easily be noted down, but journaling with feeling will have so much impact. The thoughts and emotions are the details that will fade from memory long before

your pictures, so it is important to keep a record of them – not just your own feelings, but perhaps those of the subjects on your pages as well.

Even using single words will prompt the memory of that day's events and bring it all flooding back. Add your personal handwriting to this, and you will be creating a piece of your own history, more precious than any other heirloom

The Day The

September 11th 2001

hope

GMT

1240   The Federal Aviation Administration alerted NORAD that American Airlines Flight 11 had been hijacked.

1243   FAA notified NORAD that United Airlines Flight 175 had also been hijacked.

1246   At the height of New York s morning rush hour American Airlines Flight 11 crashed into the north tower of the World Trade Centre.

1303   News cameras trained on the burning tower captured the horrifying view of another passenger jet, United Airlines Flight 175, crashing into the south tower of the Trade Centre causing a devastating explosion.

1320   The FBI announced that it was investigating reports of planes being hijacked.

1329   Rescue workers and fire fighters rush to the foot of the World Trade Centre as the upper floors blazed. On an ordinary day, up to 50,000 people would be working in the Trade Centre.

1330   A grim faced President Bush declared: We have had a national tragedy. Two aeroplanes have crashed into the World Trade Centre in an apparent terrorist attack on our country.

1340   American Airlines Flight 77, carrying 64 people from Washington to Los Angeles, crashed into the Pentagon in Washington.

1345   The White House and The Capitol were evacuated amid further threats.

1350   All airports across the US were shut down and all commercial flights grounded.

The Day the Sky Fell

Designer: Natalie O'Shea

If you want to record an historic event, find an internet site with news footage from the day and use it to make a list of events as they happened.

Sky Fell .

Hope

1358   An emergency despatcher in Pennsylvania
        receives a call from a passenger on United
        Flight 93 who says: We are being hijacked,
        we are being hijacked! Several passengers
        called relatives and told them they intend
        to try to overpower the terrorists.

1403   United Airlines Flight 93 crashed 80 miles
        south east of Pittsburgh It had been
        bound from San Francisco from Newark,
        New Jersey.

1404   The south tower of the World Trade Centre
        suddenly collapsed sending a massive ball
        of smoke across Manhattan Many emergency
        workers and fire fighters were crushed, as
        well as all those who could not get out of
        the tower.

1429   The north tower of the World Trade Centre
        collapsed aswell, adding to the devastation
        and loss of life. The southern part of Manhattan
        Island was covered in a thick layer of debris
        and dust.

1629   President Bush made a second statement, in
        which he vowed to hunt down and punish those
        responsible.

1744   The Pentagon deployed five battleships and
        two aircraft carriers along the east coast of
        the US to provide upgraded air defence from the
        New York and Washington areas.

2120   Number 7, World Trade Centre, a 47 storey
        Building adjacent to the ruins of the twin towers
        collapsed

0030   President Bush addressed the nation on TV and
        hinted at a strong US response against the
        terrorists who committed these acts and those
        who harbour them

heat gun

inkpads

foam stamps

embossing powders

rubber stamps

inking pen

embossing inkpad

wood-backed stamp

HEAT it craft tool

Stamping and Embossing

Stamping and embossing provide the opportunity to add pattern and texture to your work. They can be used alone or combined with other techniques to embellish your scrapbook pages. The handmade quality of stamped or embossed work means that a personal touch will be added to the page, whether you expect it or not.

Stamps are available in a huge range of designs, so the main problem will be choosing which ones to buy. Embossed elements can range from bold to elegant, and the addition of dimension will introduce shadow and texture to your work. There are a number of ways in which your stamps and embossing can be used to produce creative effects, so try experimenting with these techniques to produce accents that combine color and interest to enhance and complement your pictures.

Stamps

These are available both mounted and unmounted. Mounted stamps are permanently attached to a wood or acrylic block with a cushion in between. They are ready to use immediately, but it is recommended that you "condition" a new stamp with stamp cleaner before using it for the first time. This removes any deposits remaining from the manufacturing process and helps to produce a clear impression.

Mounted stamps can be bulky, which can present a challenge for storage. They should ideally be stored flat and preferably no more than two stamps high, as the weight of stamps upon each other may compress the foam cushion and produce deformation.

Unmounted stamps are considerably cheaper than mounted ones. They are available as whole sheets comprising multiple images or as trimmed individual images. Unmounted stamps can be permanently or temporarily attached to blocks to enable you to stamp an impression.

To mount a stamp permanently, attach the reverse of the stamp to some adhesive foam backing sheet (available from most craft stores). Trim the backing sheet close to the image, taking care not to cut into the image or to cut the foam away from under the stamp. Undercutting the foam from the edge of the stamp will prevent pressure being transferred to the image and can result in an incomplete stamped image. Remove the release paper from the remaining side of the backing sheet and attach the stamp to a block of wood or acrylic.

To mount a stamp temporarily, attach it to an acrylic block or other smooth surface using a glue stick. Place the card or paper to be stamped onto a mouse mat or telephone directory before stamping. These surfaces will "give" when pressure is applied to the stamp, resulting in a clean image. To remove the stamp from the block, peel it away and rinse with warm water.

Stamping

Apply ink to the entire surface of the stamp – holding the stamp face up and tapping the inkpad over the design is an easy way to check that the coverage is even. Stamp on a firm, flat surface, applying even pressure to the whole surface of the stamp. Do not slam the stamp onto the card or paper, as this can cause the stamp to bounce and shift. To achieve good results with larger stamps, try standing up to apply the pressure. Avoid moving or rocking the stamp, as this can produce a blurred or double image.

Cleaning

Stamps should be cleaned thoroughly after use and between each ink color. This will prevent inkpads from becoming tainted with previous colors and will keep the ink color consistent. Commercial stamp cleaners are available and are quick and easy to use. Blot off excess ink from the stamp before applying the stamp cleaner. Use a paper towel to absorb ink and cleaner from the stamp surface, and do not rub, as this can cause lint to be transferred to the stamp, making images blurred.

Stubborn ink residue can be removed by rubbing the stamp surface over a stamp cleaning pad or kitchen sponge. Some inks will stain stamps, leaving

This double ended embossing pen is perfect for embossed lettering.

a permanent discoloration over the surface that cannot be removed with stamp cleaner. This will not affect the quality of the image produced and is often an indication of high-quality ink.

Stamps can also be cleaned with baby-wipes, though these should be alcohol-free to prevent the stamp surface from becoming brittle. Water and dishwashing liquid provide a cheap way to clean up, but take care not to soak the foam cushion, as this may adversely affect the adhesive.

Ink pads

There are four basic types of inks available for use with rubber stamps. Pigment inks are water-based, acid-free inks that lend themselves to bright, vivid colors that are fade resistant. The formulations of these inks are slow-drying, which makes them ideal for use with embossing powders.Dye inks are water based and permanent when used on paper. They dry quickly and can sometimes bleed or feather when used on absorbent paper.

Permanent inks come in both water-soluble and solvent-based formulations. Solvent-based inks dry very fast, and do not run, bleed, or fade. They can be used to stamp onto a range of surfaces including glass, ceramic, and metal.

Clear/tinted embossing pads are not, strictly speaking, inks, though they produce a watermark-type image on any color of cardstock or paper. The glycerine-based fluids used with these pads are slow drying. Embossing powders can be applied while the ink is still wet to produce raised images.

Stamping on velvet

Beautiful effects can be produced using stamps and velvet fabric. Choose velvet that has a high silk or rayon content for best results, and select a stamp with a bold design for maximum impact. Try using this method to produce rich, ornate embellishments for your scrapbook.

Stamping on velvet

1 Turn your iron to medium/high heat and place your stamp on a firm, flat surface with the design side uppermost. Place the velvet over the stamp with the pile side down. Lightly dampen the fabric using a fine water spray,

2 Place the iron directly onto the fabric and keep it there for 15 seconds. Lift the iron and check the fabric – the impression of the stamp should be visible on the wrong side (facing you).

3 If the image cannot be seen, replace the iron for a further 5 seconds before checking again. Remove the fabric from the stamp and allow it to cool. The stamped impression will now be permanently stamped into the pile.

Soot stamping

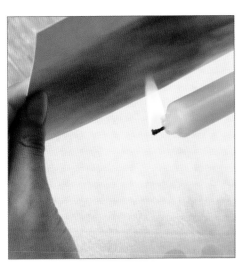

1 Hold a piece of light-colored cardstock over a candle flame, allowing the flame to coat the surface of the card with an even layer of soot. Be sure to keep the card moving or it will scorch.

2 Place the sooty card onto a firm, flat surface. Breathe over the surface of a clean stamp before pressing the stamp onto the soot on the card. Carefully lift the stamp from the card.

3 The slightly damp surface of the stamp will have removed soot to produce a light-colored stamped image on a dark background. Set the soot on the card with a sealant spray designed for chalks and pastels.

Soot stamping

This technique can be used for producing soft, subtle images that have a look of age, for creating titles (using alphabet stamps), or for journaling directly onto the page without the need for inks. The soot can be easily disturbed by handling, so be sure to hold the card by the edges only. Use a sealant to extend the life of your image. Hair spray is a readily available alternative fixative, but always use in an outside area to avoid inhaling the spray.

Embossing

This term includes any technique that raises or lowers the surface of card or paper. It can be achieved by using embossing powders and a heat gun or a template and stylus. The two techniques produce very different results, both of which can be equally stunning.

Embossing powders are fine-colored powders that melt when heat is applied. They are available in a range of colors and finishes to complement any style of layout. Fine embossing powders can be used for intricate work, while ultra-thick varieties are available that produce a glassy finish that coats and covers. Use embossing powders together with stamps or alone to produce glossy dimensional results. Apply pigment ink to provide a surface for the powder to adhere to.

To emboss using embossing powder, you will need a stamp, a pigment ink pad, some embossing powder, and a heat gun. The embossing powder is available in a variety of colors and is set with hot air.

Try a resist-stamping technique to produce light-colored images on a darker background. Stamp your chosen image onto light card using clear embossing ink. Apply clear embossing powder while the ink is still wet, and shake off the excess. Set the embossing powder using a heat gun. Apply a darker shade of ink directly

7th April 1937

Wedding

Designer: Sarah Mason

Try embossing a frame for a heritage photograph to lend an elegant texture to the layout.

onto the card, rubbing the inkpad over the entire surface. Allow the ink to dry before burnishing the card surface with a paper towel. The stamped image will retain the original color of the background in contrast to the inked card surface.

Dry embossing is achieved through the use of templates, a light box, and a stylus. The templates used are normally made from brass, but plastic alternatives are available, some of which do not require the use of a light box. A range of sizes of stylus is advisable to provide options when using different grades and weights of card and paper. An empty ballpoint pen can be used as a suitable stylus for many projects.

To dry emboss an image, tape a stencil to the front of

the card or paper used. (This is important to remember when using coated or finished card, as the final result will be pushed through the stencil to the front of the card.) Check that stencils with lettering or text are attached so that the text can be read. Place the card with the stencil attached, face down on the light box. Switch the light box on, and the outline of the stencil should be visible through the reverse side of the card. Trace around the stencil with a stylus to produce the embossed effect.

Try using this technique to create delicate borders, corners, and text directly onto your pages. The dimension that this technique will add to your page is sure to catch the eye.

Dry embossing

1 Place your card under the template that you want to use. Choose the largest size of stylus possible for each section of the template.

2 With a firm, even pressure, draw around the inside of the stencil cut-outs. The design of the template will be transferred by this technique, and therefore it is not necessary to emboss the center sections of the cut-outs.

3 Carefully remove the stencil from the card to reveal the transferred design. Add color to the embossed design by placing the stencil over the right side of the embossed card and applying chalk or ink through the stencil onto the raised image.

Embossing powder

1 If the stamp is larger than your ink pad, ink it upside down. Stamp the image onto card or paper using pigment ink.

2 While the ink is still wet, shake embossing powder over the surface of the image. Tip the excess powder onto a scrap of card and reserve for reuse.

3 Set the embossing powder with a heat gun, removing the heat as soon as the powder melts. The image will be raised from the surface of the card.

tags

ribbon charms

wire words

buckles

punched numbers

colored wires

letter tags

picture frames

picture corners

Metal embellishments can add a unique and unusual feel to scrapbooking projects, contributing texture, mood, and visual impact. Adding metal to your work can produce results that are impressive yet relatively inexpensive. An increasing interest in natural materials has made metals very popular, and the ideas in this chapter can help you to incorporate metal into any project, whatever the theme.

Metals don't have to be harsh – they can also be soft and pretty, depending on what you do with them. Look at all the metals that form part of the fabric of your life, and echo current fashions for metal in your scrapbook for up-to-the-minute pages. Look back to the past, too, for a nostalgic feel. Old metal kitchen utensils were painted in wonderful colors that were so evocative of the era – try to match these for metal embellishments that match these times and your photographs.

Ready to wear

There is such a huge range of readymade metal scrapbook embellishments available that there is certain to be something to suit all tastes. Search out words, phrases, and individual alphabet letters to add metal to your journaling. Available in a range of finishes, including copper, pewter, and aluminum, there are metals to suit most color schemes.

Products generally found in the hardware store have been reproduced for scrapbooking. Ornate keyholes, hinges, and keys can now be added to your work safely. Some of these products are purely decorative; others, such as hinges, can also be very useful.

Charms that would not look out of place on a bracelet are available in a range of metals. These can be found in craft stores together with bead specialty stores. Look at pendants and fashion jewelry for other sources of metal charms that can be added to your work. Some more unusual metal embellishments can now be found for inclusion in your projects. Ultra-thin metal stickers can add a metallic look and feel without contributing weight. Zip-pulls are also available to add a funky yet comfortable feel to layouts. Take a good look around your craft and scrapbook stores to find a host of products with a metallic feel.

The passion for incorporating metals into scrapbooks has developed to the point that metal albums are also available. These cool, clean-looking albums are surprisingly lightweight and work particularly well with contemporary designs. Unusual albums made of products such as metal are ideal when you want to create high-impact projects.

Altered alchemy

Some of the fun aspects of using a metal embellishment are the unique qualities it possesses. These can be exploited to change a metal element into something unusual or artistic. Commercially produced items can be sanded with fine-grit abrasive paper to reveal the underlying metal, which often has different qualities to the finished surface. The base metal may be a different color or have a high shine – you won't know until you experiment. If you are nervous about trying this technique, try sanding a place that will not be seen, perhaps the underside or an edge. Using this technique, cool pewter can be changed to warm copper or something equally exciting, increasing the range of color schemes in which the product can be used.

The use of acrylic paint can change a sleek,

You can change the style of metal plaques, and alter the color, by using sandpaper to give a softer look

sophisticated metal item into a soft, shabby, chic embellishment. Choose a paint color to complement your theme and apply to the metal surface. Allow it to dry before applying a second coat, if required. The painted surface can be further altered by sanding to produce an aged, worn look. Lightly rub fine-grit abrasive paper over edges, corners, and raised sections to reveal glimpses of metal and reproduce the effects of age. If used over silver or aluminum, the finished result will resemble old painted tin.

If you do not like the timeworn look, you could try a more subtle effect that is also achieved by altering the painted finish. When the paint is dry, rub a finger over the surface of a metallic rub-on cream. Gently brush your finger over the painted surface of your item, and the cream will adhere to any edges and raised decoration. Continue until you are happy with the effect, which will instantly add a little history to the piece.

Metal elements can become unique pieces by alteration using stamps. A solvent-based permanent ink pad will produce a clear image on a metal surface, and these are available in a range of colors. Individual alphabet stamps can be used to create journaling directly onto metal that is personal or pertinent to your photographs. Images can be stamped onto any relatively flat metal surface, and no two pieces will ever be the same. Combine a number of stamps to produce a collage effect, which can be fresh and fun or intriguing and artistic.

You could try using a patinating fluid to change the color of some or all of the metal surface. These fluids react with the metal to tarnish it rapidly. They can be applied with a brush or can be used with stamps to give great results (but make sure the stamps are cleaned

Wire word

1 Start by writing out the word on paper. Practice until you are happy with the results and can follow the lettering with a single piece of wire.

2 To make a wire word, cut a length of wire and begin to bend it, following the lines of your word, using round nose pliers. Continue until the word or letter is complete.

immediately to prevent any degradation of the surface).

Metals can also be altered without applying any other medium, simply by the application of heat. When trying this technique, use pliers or tweezers with insulated handles to hold the metal piece securely. Place the metal directly into the flame of a gas stove or other similar heat source. Exploit some of the properties of metal by heating it until the surface changes color slightly. This produces an iridescent finish that can be subtle or dramatic, depending on the type of metal heated. Thinner metals may soften when heated and can produce interesting effects. Try dipping hot metal directly into an embossing powder – it will be coated with a thick layer of enamel that will set immediately. This technique can reproduce the effect of solder.

Do it yourself

If you cannot find the perfect metal addition to your scrapbook, there is always the option to make something from scratch. Some scrapbook manufacturers produce thin metal sheets that can be used in die-cut systems to

make any shape, including tags and lettering. These sheets are often thin enough to be cut with craft scissors to produce freehand designs. Thin metal can also be stamped into using metal stamping dies for a different take on journaling.

You could try cutting thin strips of metal about $3/8$ in. (9 mm) wide and feeding these into an embossed label maker. These machines give the freedom to combine any numbers or letters, making thin strips of raised text that make great additions to your work. Rub a solvent-based ink pad over the embossed text to contrast against the metal, so making the raised lettering more legible.

Change the color of your metal to match your layout by using acrylic paints. Enhance the embellishment by applying metallic rub-ons gently over the painted surface.

3 Thread beads onto the wire and distribute them randomly along contours of your word or shape.

4 Cut off the excess wire and bend back the cut end. Attach the word to your work with adhesive or by making U-shaped pins from thin wire and wrapping these around the wire word before securing each one with a twist on the back.

Leah and Daisy

Designer: Mandy Webb

Try cutting tags from the various different metal-effect papers available, for a unique and shiny look.

Look around your hardware store for inspiration for more metallic scrapbook embellishments. Screen mesh can be used as a background for a page or border. The soft mesh can be frayed for a shabby-chic style, or wrapped around firm card to give a sleek, smart finish. Try pinning, stapling, or tying smaller items to the mesh to create titles, journaling, or decorative elements. Heavier-grade mesh such as chicken wire evokes a country feel when used on a scrapbook project. Try layering chicken wire over patterned paper for a fun look reminiscent of antique kitchen cupboards. Experiment with wire mesh as a photo mount. Begin by cutting a piece of mesh about 1/2 in. (12 mm) larger all around than your photograph. Set a eyelet in each of the corners of the photo, and attach the picture to the mount with small pieces of thin wire. If you want to get more creative, change the color of the mesh with a permanent marker or by heating and dipping it in embossing powder. Mesh is such a versatile item that you could challenge yourself to create an entire layout using mesh and metal – the effect can be stunning.

Look at wire in both the hardware store and craft store for a range of gauges. The higher the gauge of wire, the thinner it will be. Fine-gauge wire can be manipulated easily with your hands, but thicker gauges may require pliers to bend them.

Use wire to make words or letters for embellishing your projects. Start by writing the word or letter on paper without taking your pen off the paper. This might sound simple enough, but it can be tricky when you need to dot an i or cross a t. With a little perseverance you will be able to create words, letters, and numbers freehand.

Beads and wire are a great combination, because the wire can be bent into abstract shapes and the beads

can add visual excitement. Thread beads onto thin gauge wire and bend it into shapes such as flowers, butterflies, or dragonflies. Stretch beaded wire across your pages to add a pretty, linear accent to your work.

Stick to it

Metal can be challenging to adhere to scrapbook pages. Strong adhesives are required to permanently attach these elements to card or paper, particularly as they are slightly heavier than many items used in scrapbooking.

Metal adhesives are designed specifically for this purpose. These are wet glues that form a strong bond with metals. Apply an even coat of adhesive to the back of the metal before adhering it to the page. Leave the glue to dry completely before adding the page to your album.

Try using adhesive dots to attach metals. These small dots of glue transfer easily to metal surfaces and require no drying time. Larger metal items will require a number of dots evenly spaced over the surface to minimize stress on your background card.

A glue stick is ideal for small, lightweight metal items. Coat the back of the item with glue and press down firmly to ensure good adhesion. The adhesive will require a little drying time before it can be moved or stored, especially if the surface is raised.

Glazes can also be used for metal embellishments, as these are strong adhesives. Metals can be coated with glaze and adhered in one step to give a high shine that firmly holds the item in place. Glazes require quite a long drying time, so set your work aside and do not be tempted to touch it, especially if you want a smooth shiny result.

Boy

Designer: Alison McGovern

Create a co-ordinated look by using different embellishments in the same color metal.

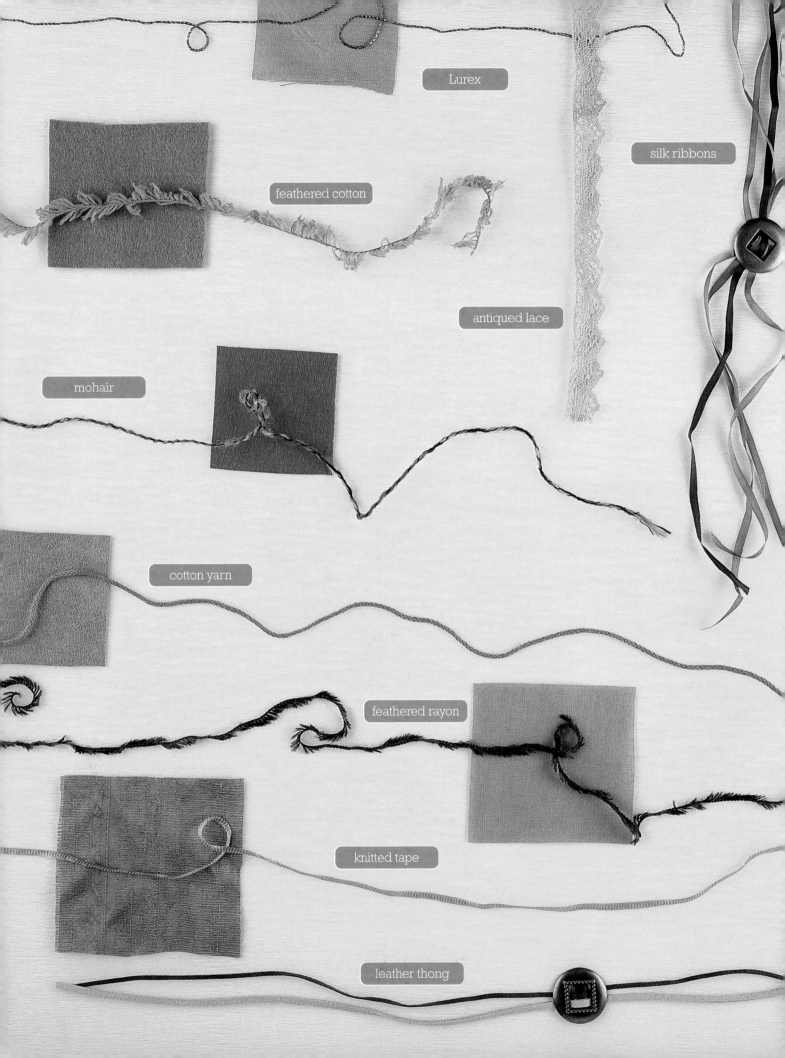

Lurex

silk ribbons

feathered cotton

antiqued lace

mohair

cotton yarn

feathered rayon

knitted tape

leather thong

Fabric and Fibers

Including fabric and ribbon can add interesting colors, patterns, and textures to your scrapbook pages. And the needlework techniques you can use to attach these items will help to create beautiful pages that are visually interesting. Stitching, whether by hand or machine, can add to the overall design and emphasize the theme.

A craft store or fabric store will reveal a host of ribbons, braids, and other decorative trims that can be incorporated into scrapbook designs. Look around at textiles and fabrics and the different ways they can be combined to find inspiration for your own work. Then challenge yourself to complete a project putting these new ideas into practice.

the fabric and the surrounding page elements. This may be something that you are prepared to risk, although you could face a rather nasty shock in a few years' time.

Look through the sale bins at fabric stores, where there are often small pieces of very expensive, beautiful fabrics on offer at very affordable prices. Even a small amount of fabric can be used to great effect in a page design. Furnishing stores often offer free swatches of furnishing fabrics. These are a perfect size for creating patchwork backgrounds or embellishing tags. Fabric sample books are regularly discontinued and contain larger pieces of fabric suitable for backgrounds. Ask at your local stores and you may find many of these available to you for no cost at all.

Rather than purchasing fabric, how about using items of clothing? The patterns and designs of clothing

Opposite: There are many different kinds of fibers, fabrics, threads, and yarns available (see page 78).

Fairy Tale Castle
Designer: Alison Docherty
Use pieces of old curtains or upholstery fabric on your layout to give your page an extra dimension.

Fabric

Most fabric is completely safe to use in your scrapbook. The acid and lignin-free aspect concerning paper is not an issue here, since fabrics are not a product of wood and are not usually processed with acid. The only textiles to be wary of are leather, suede, and vinyl. Leather and suede are chemically processed, and there may possibly be residual chemicals in the end product. If you find a piece of suede or leather that would be perfect for a project, decide how important it is to you and the photographs that it is totally safe. Some craft manufacturers produce leather embellishments for scrapbooks that are safe to use, and these may be an alternative to consider.

Vinyls include plastics that are volatile (they give off a distinctive odour). The chemicals given off by these volatile plastics are not conducive to the preservation of your photographs, and so should be avoided. Check the label on the roll or ask an assistant for details of the composition of any fabric before you purchase it.

Check textiles for metallic threads. These are not treated and can corrode, discoloring both

Beautiful Memories

Designer: Karen McIvor

Fabric swatches sewn together as a background for your page create a soft, subtle feel and look that perfectly evokes the era of the photograph.

are one of the things that capture the feel of an era. Match some fabric to your photographs, and produce a design that is in keeping with that time. Look through your closet before you bag clothes up for the thrift store, and think about ways you could include them in your album. If you are reluctant to cut up something, it could always be scanned and the design printed onto cardstock as an alternative.

Look through your craft box for scraps of fabric from other projects. That small scrap of lace from a baby dress, the fabric left over from shortening pants, and the pocket from an old pair of jeans can all be used to create something for next to nothing. These items will have the extra value of the memories attached to the original clothing, making them perfect for an album full of memories. Include a photograph of a subject wearing these clothes, and the theme is already planned for you.

Ribbons, braids, and lace

Like fabrics, most ribbons, braids, and lace are safe to use on your pages. But be sure to check for wire edging and metallic threads, as these can both tarnish.

Ribbons provide a very simple way to create a border for your page. Attach an end to the reverse of the background cardstock before laying it across the front of the design. Ensure that the ribbon is straight before attaching the remaining end to the reverse. Be a little more creative by adding a knot or a bow, and this becomes a feature in itself.

Thread ribbon through buckles, ribbon charms, or rings to make interesting elements for your page, or attach it to the back of mounted photographs to create a hanger. Ribbon can also be used to make photo corners: wrap a short piece of ribbon around a corner of a picture and attach the ends on the reverse.

French knotting

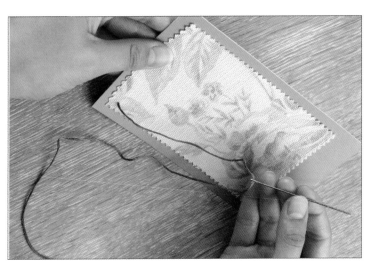

1 Place the fabric on your project and hold it in place with a little temporary adhesive. Pierce a hole through the fabric and card. Tie a simple knot on the end of your thread, and pass your needle through the hole from the wrong side.

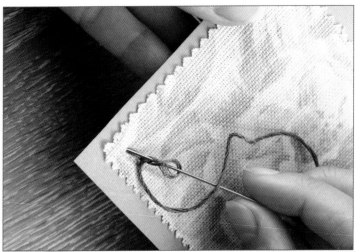

2 Wrap your thread around the needle in a figure of eight, before passing the needle back through the hole.

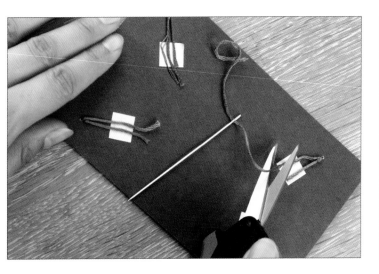

3 This will make a decorative knot on top of your work. Secure the remaining thread end on the wrong side using double-sided, or photosafe tape and trim off the ends.

4 Repeat as necessary, making knots in all four corners of a square, for instance, to secure it to the background. Cutting the fabric with pinking shears will stop it fraying.

Thread lengths of coordinating ribbons through a tag or even through a hole in a photo mount to create layers of texture that catch the eye. You could also use ribbon to tie mini-books or bundles of tags together.

You will find braids in both haberdashery and upholstery stores. The range of colors, textures, and sizes available is huge. Look for end-of-line sales for bargains. Examine how braids are used on home furnishings, and duplicate these looks on your pages. For example, braid from the edge of a throw could become braid around a photo mount. If you see braid or other decorative trimmings on an eye-catching home décor project that inspires you, ask if you can take a photo of it; otherwise you can make a few notes and a quick sketch to jog your memory later.

White lace can be antiqued easily (see below), the result will be a lovely colored lace that looks as though it has been around for years.

Fibers

These are inexpensive decorative yarns that can be used to add interesting color and texture to your work. They are available in a number of different types and can be found in the knitting yarn section of craft stores. New yarns are constantly being developed and produced, so keep an eye out for new arrivals in store.

Some unusual fibers may be more difficult to source than others. Try searching the Internet for particular fiber types or interesting colors. Many suppliers stock these in small craft lengths, saving the expense of buying a whole ball.

Use your fibers for ties and bindings or in a bundle through the top of a tag. Try sewing with fibers or wrapping them around the bottom of a photograph to draw attention to it. Mix fibers, fabric, and ribbons in small or large quantities – the possibilities are endless.

Staining with tea

1 White lace trimmings can be given a feeling of age and antiquity by being stained to produce a soft creamy color. Make a cup of tea or coffee to normal strength and set it aside to cool slightly. Place a length of lace in the tea or coffee and leave it to steep.

2 Check the color after 5 minutes, and return the lace to the liquid if the color has not developed sufficiently. Keep checking at 5-minute intervals until the desired color is achieved. Remove the lace from the cup and rinse in clear cold water before setting it aside to dry.

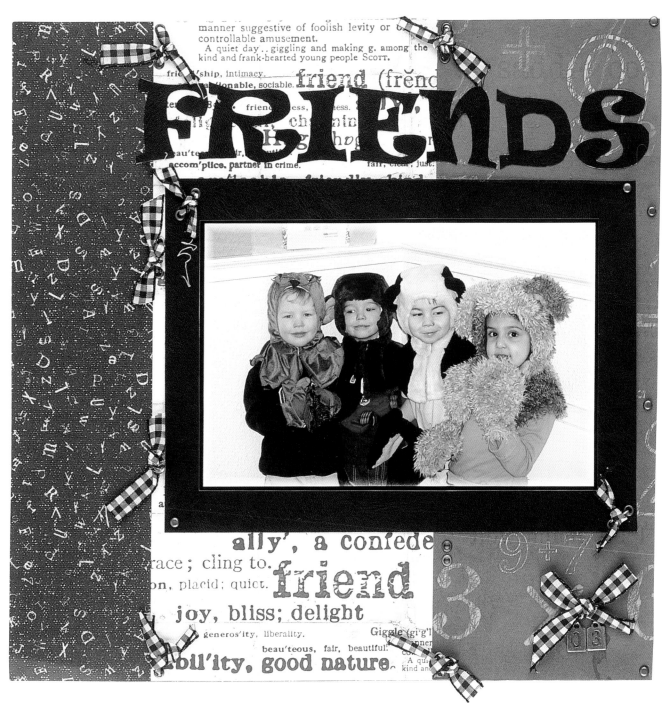

Friends

Designer: Alison McGovern

Ribbons are used here as a fun way to attach layers together.

Sew and sew

Some glues can make fabrics rigid, thereby changing one of the properties that make them an attractive choice for inclusion in your work. One way to avoid this is to sew them in place instead. Even the simplest of stitches can be used to great effect, and no great skill with a needle is needed for this (see French knot technique on page 75). Cardstock and paper can be easily stitched using a large needle with a straight eye. Piercing the paper before stitching can help to make this a quick method of attaching fabric to your work.

Place the fabric on your project and hold it in place with a little temporary adhesive. Using a piercing tool or needle, pierce holes through the fabric and background cardstock at regular intervals. The distance between the holes will affect the size of the finished stitching. Knot your thread end, and beginning at the back of your work, start to stitch through each of the holes to produce a simple running stitch. If a knot will make an unsightly bump in the page, use tape to hold the ends.

Two parallel lines of pierced holes will enable you to cross-stitch, whip stitch, or blanket stitch the fabric in place. Any fancy stitch can be used to match the theme or mood of your photographs.

A row of knots can be as effective decoratively and practically as a row of stitches, so try using French knots to hold the fabric in place, one in each corner.

Scrapbook pages can be stitched using a sewing machine for really fast results without the need to pre-pierce holes. Use a scrap of fabric and card together to test for tension and stitch length. Adjust your machine to produce even stitches that are not too close together: close stitching can tear through the card and will be ineffective.

Once your machine has been set up, you are ready to sew anything you choose. A straight stitch will give a simple, clean finish that will work with any project. Use a zigzag stitch where layers of fabric overlap and over raw edges to prevent fraying. You could even use a buttonhole stitch and attach layers of fabric and cardstock using buttons. Within reason, whatever you can do with fabric, you should be able to reproduce with cardstock and fabric together.

No-sew methods

If the idea of sewing does not appeal, there are other ways to attach fabrics and ribbons to your pages. Run lengths of ribbon or pieces of fabric through a Xyron® machine. The adhesive will not stiffen the material and will be evenly applied to the edges to minimize fraying. Xyron® is a very effective method of attaching sheer fabrics and ribbon, and is virtually invisible (see page 35).

Adhesive dots will firmly hold the ends of ribbon or braid in place. If the ribbon or braid passes to the reverse of the work, attach the ends there for an invisible finish. If you want to attach a small piece of fabric to a page, place glue dots at the corners.

For other fast fixes without stitching, fabrics and braids can be attached with eyelets, brads, and snaps. You could even continue the needlework theme by using dressmaker's pins as attachments—pin from the front of your work to produce a neat and simple fixing. This works equally well using small safety pins, which also have the advantage of leaving no sharp points.

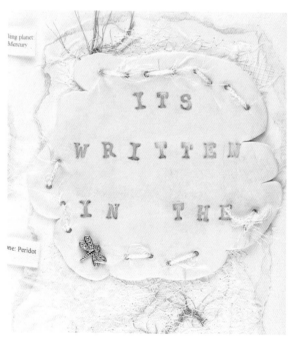

*A detail of handsewing on paper as used for **Its Written in the Stars** by Dawn Inskip, in the Family Chapter.*

Making a wedding blessing

This is a delightful and memorable way to invite people to your wedding – a token they will treasure, and perhaps use in their scrapbooking albums later.

1 Print out your invite card, and with a craft knife and self-healing cutting mat, remove the letter B from the center of the card.

2 Cut out two heart shapes in the same color card. These will replace the centers of the letter.

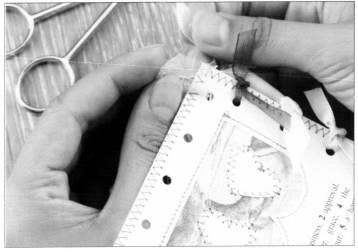

3 Place decorative fabric or paper behind the card. Using a zig-zag machine stitch, work around the edges. Outline the letter using a straight stitch. Hold the hearts in place with light adhesive, and then stitch the hearts in a zigzag.

4 Using a single hole-punch, make holes at regular intervals around the edges of the card. Use small snippets of fine ribbon to add the finishing touch.

paint

archival pens

sponge brushes

chalks

metallic rub-ons

powdered color

chalks

metallic pens

Paint, Chalk, Ink, and Rub-ons

If the color, finish, or effect you want to achieve is not available ready-printed on patterned cardstock or paper, produce these effects for yourself with paint, chalk, ink, or rub-ons. These can be used alone or combined together to produce inspired scrapbook pages that get people asking, "How did you do that?"

These materials can add color to your work in so many different ways that you could probably use them on any number of pages without achieving the same result twice. Use brushes, applicators, and even your fingers to add a creative finish to any scrapbook pages.

Paints

Watercolor and acrylic paints are safe to use in your scrapbook, and produce quite different results.

Watercolor paints are available in dry cake form or tubes of cream color. The addition of varying amounts of water produces colors of different intensity, but watercolors are usually soft, delicate colors that are easy on the eye. The high water content of the mixed watercolor paint can cause scrapbook card and paper to warp and buckle if used over large areas. If this is a concern, use acid-free watercolor paper, which has been pre-treated to minimize buckling and is widely available.

Create backgrounds for your layouts by painting broad stripes on your paper with watercolors. Mixing wet watercolors on the page produces soft, graduated color changes that can make beautiful blended backgrounds or photo mounts.

You can make delicately patterned paper using watercolors and a household candle. Use the candle as you would a pencil to draw simple designs such as a flower over a clean sheet of paper, then paint over the entire surface with watercolor paint. The paint will only adhere to the unwaxed paper, while the design will remain the color of the underlying paper. Leave the paint to dry before trimming the paper to use on your page. You can also use watercolors to add color to stamped images. Use a solvent-based ink to stamp the image, then allow it to dry. Use paints to add detail to the image – a little is often all that is required. Stamped and embossed images can be colored in the same way, and the embossing powder will prevent other types of ink from running when the paint is applied.

If you are particularly artistic, you could paint scenes or elements from your photographs to use as accents or embellishments.

Acrylic paint is available in tubes and bottles and has a high pigment content. These vibrant colors can be diluted with water to thin them before use. Unlike watercolor, acrylic paint will become permanent when it has dried. Acrylics can be used to produce a dry-brush finish on your cardstock. Using a clean foam or bristle brush, pick up a little paint across the tip of the brush. Brush the tip onto a piece of paper towel until nearly all the paint has been removed, then lightly brush the color onto a clean piece of cardstock. Work in even strokes, building up the effect slowly. Remember, you can always add more paint but you cannot take it away. This technique can be used on a whole sheet of card or just around the edges to give a soft weathered look. Paint two pieces of card at the same time to make additional materials for co-ordinating elements such as tags and journaling boxes.

Combine acrylic paints and crackle glazes (available from craft stores) to produce a cracked-paint effect with a feeling of age. Follow the instructions on the crackle glaze to obtain the best results.

Acrylic paints have a wonderful creamy consistency that makes them a good stamping medium. Use them with rubber and foam stamps to make titles, embellishments, and journaling. Foam stamps have an affinity with acrylic paint that gives lovely results. Look for foam stamps with bold designs, as these give the best results with paint. Pour a little paint into a tray, and use a brush to load the stamp to ensure that it is evenly covered. Place the stamp firmly on the card or paper, then lift it off and set the paper aside to dry. (The paint can cause the stamp to slip on the surface, so ensure that the stamp is placed straight on the card and lifted off vertically.) Clean your stamps with water immediately after use.

Try stamping after attaching layers of card to your design – the paint will unite the layers visually, creating a unifying theme. If you are feeling brave, try stamping with paint over the edge or corner of a photograph for a different slant on photo corners. Otherwise, simulate this effect by stamping onto a transparency and trimming it to produce corners.

Acrylic paint can also be used on metal, ceramic, and other embellishments, but some surfaces with a highly polished finish may require a light sanding before the paint is applied. Acrylic paint dries quite quickly, and additional coats of paint can be applied as required. These paints give good coverage, and it is rare that more than two coats are necessary.

Chalks

These are an easy and wonderful way to add touches of subtle color to your scrapbook, and any mistakes can be removed with a pencil eraser. Craft chalks are available in palettes of colors and are acid-free. Use an applicator to apply the chalks, because your fingers will be slightly acidic and this can transfer to the colors. Applicators also minimize mess, since color changes are as simple as picking up another applicator, and there is no chance of color being transferred by your fingers.

Use chalks to highlight torn edges of card or paper and tone down the stark contrast of a white core. You can also use them to color the edges of light-colored card to give a feeling of depth to the design.

One of the most dramatic uses for chalks is in producing extended backgrounds to photographs. This technique works best with pictures that include horizons and scenery, such as beach and seascapes. Begin by attaching your photograph in the center of a sheet of white card. Look carefully to see where the horizon runs off the edge of the picture, and use chalk in the same color to extend this onto the background card. Draw the horizon across the page on both sides of the photograph.

Use chalks to color the sky above the horizon, matching the color and adding clouds or other details

Wax resist

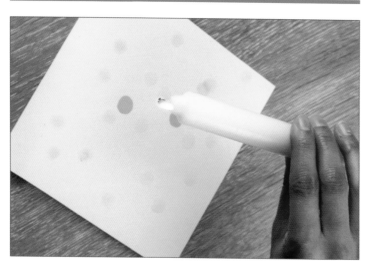

1 Light an ordinary household candle, and drip the wax in drops over your paper, being careful not to burn your hands.

2 The wax will set almost immediately, so use a watered down wash of paint and flood the background. The paint will not take where the wax is, allowing the pattern to show through.

tre e Together

Great things are not
done by impulse,
but by a series of small
things brought together.
-Vincent Van Gogh

FAMILY

together together together together together together together together

Family

Designer: Karen McIvor

Change the color of wooden letters by painting them. Chalk or paint the edges to match your color scheme.

from the picture. Then use another chalk to match the color below the horizon, and fill in this area on either side of the photograph. Note how the colors in the picture change, and reproduce this with your chalks. Using this technique, a small photograph can be extended to become a whole page in your album, making it a simple way to produce a stunning page.

Chalk pastels are another option. (Take care not to purchase oil pastels, which are a completely different product.) Chalk pastels are usually produced in small sticks in a rainbow of shades and colors. To prevent the transfer of oils and acid from the fingers during use, leave them in the box and pick up the color with an applicator or cotton swab. Chalks and pastels are fragile and can easily break, so treat them carefully.

Inks

Calligraphy inks can be used together with a dip pen for journaling. What better way to include your handwriting in your album than by writing across a whole sheet of card or paper to produce a background paper? Practice calligraphy to create titles, journaling, or accents that will say exactly what you want in whatever style, size, or color you choose.

Calligraphy inks are produced in a range of intense colors, including pearlized and metallic. If you are unsure of your penmanship, then you could try painting these inks onto paper. Drops, splashes, and dribbles of ink can give really interesting results that would be ideal for school-themed pages, for example.

Walnut ink is made by boiling black walnuts to produce a dark brown ink. This is available in both crystal and, less commonly, liquid form. Just add a tablespoon (15 ml) of the crystals to a cup of hot water to reconstitute and create the ink. Walnut ink gives a wonderful, aged look to card or paper and can be used in a number of ways. Dip sheets of card or paper into the ink, ensuring that the whole surface is covered with ink before removing and setting the card or paper aside to dry. The finished result will be mottled and uneven, much like a piece of old weathered paper (see page 85).

Alter the finished effect by sprinkling salt grains onto the card or paper while it is still wet. The salt will absorb the ink and reproduce "foxing" – the dark spots that appear on paper over time.

For a color change that is lighter and easier to control, spray walnut ink onto the surface of some card using a fine water-spray bottle. Keep adding layers of color in this way to achieve the desired effect.

Paint walnut ink onto card using smooth brushstrokes to give a relatively even color, or stipple the brush onto the surface for more texture. Allowing ink to drip from the end of the paintbrush produces puddles of ink that dry a darker color. Use an old toothbrush to apply ink for a coarser look, or flick the ink from the bristles for tiny droplets.

Crumpling the card or paper before applying the ink will produce broken paper fibers that are more absorbent. The crumpled look will be accentuated by the ink and give a antiqued appearance to the final piece.

Metallic Rub-ons

These are a great way to add accent color. They are pigments suspended in a waxy cream base and are available in palettes containing a selection of colors.

Metallic rub-ons are applied with the finger and rubbed onto the surface of card, paper, ceramic, wood, and other hard surfaces. They can be used to give subtle color variations or add a metallic sheen. Try the color on a scrap of paper before applying it to the surface, as the pigments can vary in intensity.

Use metallic rub-ons to highlight dry embossed images, rubbing the color lightly over the surface. This will highlight the raised elements of the design, making it more prominent.

Rub color over painted finishes to make the colors softer and to give an aging effect. A textured surface will pick up the color on the raised sections of the texture, making these stand out against the background.

Aging with walnut ink

1 Mix 1 teaspoon of walnut ink crystals with 1 cup (250 ml) of hot water in a shallow dish. Stir to dissolve the crystals.

2 Crumple the card into a tight ball. The creases will absorb more ink and produce a leathery effect.

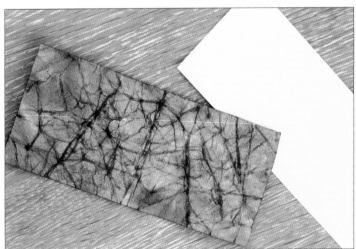

3 Unfold the card and dip it into the dish of ink. Ensure that the card is completely immersed in the ink.

4 Remove the card from the ink and set aside to dry. Once dry, the card can be ironed flat with a warm iron.

Projects

ITS
WRITTE
IN THE

Birthstone: Peridot

YEAR
OF THE
GOAT

lucky colour: white

Family

Friendships may come and go, but the love within a family lasts forever. Celebrate your family by creating pages dedicated to them.

It's Written in the Stars

Designer: Dawn Inskip

Our families are a part of what makes us who we are. These relationships are special and deserve to be recognized as such. Pictures of family occasions will create an archive that records the "who, what, where, and when" of each gathering. Families are far from static and your photographs can help to record the changes that occur within your family group.

Try using the sewing machine to stitch your fibers onto accents and cards.

Instructions

Use white card as the main background for each page.

Stitched mats

To make a stitched mat, cut a 12 in. x 6 in. (30.5 cm x 15 cm) strip of cardstock and roughly tear around all edges, tearing toward you so that rough edges are on the right side, until the piece measures approximately 10 in. x 5 in. (25.5 cm x 13 cm). The more uneven the edges, the better the effect. Chalk the rough edges. Set the sewing machine to zigzag stitch. Start by adhering the mesh to the mat.

Gradually add small lengths of fibers, fabrics, and other materials. Continue to add the fibers, fabrics, and materials until the mat is sufficiently covered.

Place four background mats as the backgrounds for your photographs.

Photo frames

Cut a piece of heavy weight card to form a frame shape around each of the photographs. Carefully cover each frame with white velvet paper, cutting and mitering the corners for a neat finish. Secure all edges on the reverse of the frame to conceal any untidiness.

Use an embossing tool and ruler to create a mitered crease in each corner of the frames. Mount the frames

MATERIALS

Heavyweight card
Velvet paper
Assorted ribbons
Assorted fibers
Charms
Brads
Spiral clips
Air-dry clay
Alphabet stamps

onto the photographs. Wrap ribbon several times around the lower section of each framed photograph, securing the ends with a knot. Attach charms to the ribbons and then adhere the framed photos to the background.

Title and journaling

Roll air-dry clay into a thin sheet and use alphabet stamps to create a title embossed in the clay sheet. Pierce holes around the edges of the clay sheet and set aside to dry.

Create letter tiles by cutting squares of clay and stamping with fancy alphabet letters.

Once the clay is dry, add color with watercolor pencils and secure the clay sheet to the background with strong adhesive. Embellish by stitching through the holes around the border. Adhere the letter tiles to the background with strong adhesive.

Computer journal onto cream card and cut into strips slightly wider than the background mats. Attach with brads across the stitched mats.

Finishing touches

Add charms and printed twill strips to finish.

Walk Along Beside me Daddy

Designer: Alison McGovern

MATERIALS

- Patterned paper
- Black card
- Co-ordinating patterned paper
- Brads
- Label maker
- Letter tiles
- Rub-on lettering
- Alphabet stamps
- Assorted charms

Here, styles of lettering have been mixed to create a page where journaling is part of the overall design.

Instructions

Use a sheet of patterned paper as the main background for your page.

Photo mount

Mount a single photograph onto black cardstock and trim a narrow border. Mount once again onto a co-ordinating patterned paper and trim a generous border. Attach the mounted photograph to the center of the background using brads.

Title and journaling

Use a label maker to create journaling and attach this to the bottom right corner of the background. Add further label maker strips across the bottom of the design.

Use letter tiles, rub-ons, and stamps to create the remaining title and journaling elements.

Finishing touches

Finish with a compass, watch face, and compass needle embellishment.

Family Memories

Designer: Mandy Webb

Red card

4 sheets of
 co-ordinating
 patterned paper

Hinges/photo flips

Ribbon charms

Buckle

Eyelets

Adhesive dots

Background

Use dark red cardstock as the main background. Cut ¼ in. (6 mm) from one side of each of three sheets of co-ordinating patterned papers and discard these extra strips. This will allow a narrow border to show all around the edges of the page.

Cut an 8 in. (20.5 cm) strip of the first paper and attach across the bottom of the background leaving an even border around the bottom and side edges. Cut a ½ in. (13 mm) strip of the second paper to be used and attach above the first piece, slightly overlapping the edge.

Attach a 4 in. (10 cm) strip of the third paper and a 1 in. (2.5 cm) strip of the final paper in the same way.

Photo mount and title

Mount a single photograph onto co-ordinating red cardstock and trim an even border. Cut 4 in. (10 cm) of ribbon, form a loop, and attach this to the reverse side of the photo mount. Attach the mounted photo to the background using photo flips. Thread word charms onto bead chain and attach through the ribbon loop. Fix to the background with adhesive dots.

Finishing touches

Thread ribbon through both sides of a buckle and fix ends using circle eyelet shapes. Attach any remaining ribbon ends to the reverse of the design.

Hinges can help create hidden spaces for journaling under your photographs.

Heritage

The older the photographs, the more important it is to archive them well for future generations to enjoy.

Family History

Designer: Mandy Webb

In the same way that we safeguard our jewels, we should be sure that we safeguard the pictures of generations of our families. The best environment for heritage photographs is in a scrapbook album. Collecting old photographs also provides an opportunity for you to learn more about the subjects to create as full and detailed a history as possible.

Nellie & William
Circa 1930

Making "Family History"

Heritage pages often use colors and patterns that are sympathetic to the style and era of the pictures to create a soft elegant feel to your layouts. Choose pale or sepia-colored lace and cards that will blend with your photographs.

MATERIALS

- Plain cardstock
- Patterned paper
- Ribbon
- Lace
- Label holders
- Metal corners
- 3-D foam pads

Instructions

Use a sheet of dark-colored cardstock as the main background for both pages of the design.

Woven panels

Make two panels of woven patterned papers following the instructions below, trim to 11 in. (28 cm) square, and attach to the center of each background.

Cut eight 12 in. x ¼ in. (30 cm x 6 mm) strips of patterned paper and attach these along the other edges of the background card to create a border.

Attach a bow centrally towards the top of each woven panel. Cut two 5 in. (13 cm) lengths of ribbon creating an angle at one end of each length. Attach these to the center of each panel with the angled end touching the bottom edge of each page.

Photo mounts

Mount each photograph onto brown cardstock and trim a narrow border. Mount again onto cream card and cut a wider border. Mount for a third time onto brown card and trim a narrow border.

Use 3-D foam pads to attach the mounted photos to the center of each woven panel, over the ribbon.

Finishing touches

Handwrite or print titles onto cream card. Trim to size and mount onto brown card, trimming a narrow border. Attach a label holder over the title using strong adhesive. Attach the title blocks under each photograph and add decorative photo corners to the bottom of each photograph to frame.

Weaving step-by-step

1 Choose 4 sheets of contrasting patterned paper, 2 light and 2 dark, and cut into 1 in. (2.5 cm) strips.

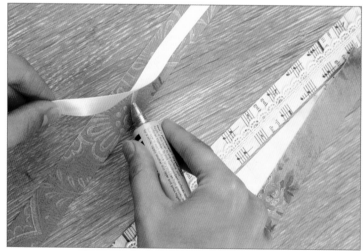

2 Choose 1 strip from each paper and glue ribbon or lace along its length.

3 Lay two dark strips side by side. Next weave a light strip under the first strip then over the second strip. Fix the end in place on the back. Carry on weaving, adding more strips as you go.

4 Randomly add the lace and ribbon strips. Complete the panel and glue the ends in place on the back. Trim to neaten the edges if needed.

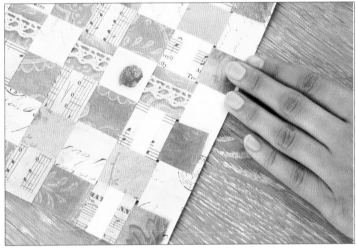

5 It is the random mix of the paper and lace that add to the charm of this type of background, so no need to plan it too carefully or it may look overworked.

Memories

Designer: Alison Docherty

MATERIALS

Dark-colored
  cardstock
Patterned paper,
Fabric remnants
Rickrack braid
Metal word tag
3-D foam tabs

Fabrics can be used in place of patterned paper to add color and texture.

Instructions

Use a single sheet of cardstock as the main background. Cut a piece of patterned paper 11½ in. x 5½ in. (29 cm x 14 cm) and attach to the left side of the background. Use a sewing machine to stitch around the edges of the patterned paper.

Cut a number of co-ordinating fabrics into rectangles 6 in. x 3 in. (15 cm x 7.5 cm) and arrange onto the background as you desire. Stitch each piece in place onto the background.

Photo mount

Mount a single photograph onto dark cardstock and trim a narrow border along the top, bottom, and left sides. Allow a 1½ in. (4 cm) border on the right side of the mount.

Cut a strip of patterned paper ¾ in. (2 cm) wide and attach to the right side of the photo mount. Cut a length of rickrack braid and slide on the metal word tag. Adhere the rickrack over the patterned paper strip on the photo mount.

Finishing touches

Attach the mounted photo to the background using 3-D foam pads.

The Bridesmaid

Designer: Alison McGovern

MATERIALS

Plain cardstock
Patterned paper
Hole punch
3-D floral
   embellishments
Alphabet stickers
Ribbon
Ribbon slide
Photo corners
Heart brads
Tag
Walnut ink
Ultra-thick
   embossing
   enamel
Rubber stamp title
Gold ink pad
Letter stickers

Instructions

Use a sheet of cardstock as the main background. Trim 1 in. (2.5 cm) from two adjacent sides of a co-ordinating colored cardstock and attach to the center of the background. Trim 1½ in. (4 cm) from two adjacent sides of a sheet of floral patterned paper and attach to the center of the background.

Using a hole punch, make 16 holes around the page along the edge where the two cardstock sheets meet. Use a brad to gather the ribbon at one corner – pass the brad either side of the ribbon, through the hole, and open the prongs on the reverse. Continue until a brad has been secured through each hole creating regular gathers around the border. Attach a single photograph to the background, offsetting it slightly to the right side of the design, and hold it in place with photo corners.

Finishing touches

Dye the tag with walnut ink and allow to dry. Melt ultra thick embossing enamel in a melt pot and dip the dry tag. Remove, and quickly stamp the tag all over with a script stamp inked with gold. When the tag has cooled, attach a 3-D floral embellishment and thread a length of ribbon through the hole. Attach a ribbon slide before tying the ribbon in a bow. Fix the tag to the left side of the design. Add a further flower to the bottom right corner of the background, slightly overlapping the photograph. Use letter stickers to create a title.

Ribbon can be used to frame a page for a soft, delicate look.

Travel

Journeys abroad can be a wonderful
inspiration for your scrapbook pages
as well as providing the photographs.

New York

Designer: Alison Docherty

Whether it is the trip of a lifetime or the annual visit to the beach, travel presents a host of opportunities to collect together items for scrapbooking. Save tickets, postcards and other mementoes that are specific to your destination. Foreign coins and stamps make great additions to scrapbook pages and can add a real feeling of place.

Making "New York"

Don't forget to take photographs that capture some of the essence of travel – piles of suitcases, or tickets and passports ready to go. Be sure to pack loads of film because you will almost certainly be taking lots of pictures. Black and white photographs perfectly portray the urban landscape of the city.

MATERIALS

Plain cardstock in
    white and three
    shades of gray
Printed sheet of
    transparency
Metal foil
Fibers
Letter charms
Brads

Background

Use a light gray card as the main background. Cut a sheet of mid gray card in half and attach one piece vertically to the left page. Cut an 8 in. (20.5 cm) piece of soft gray card and attach this to the left side of the right page. Adhere the remaining half of the mid-gray card horizontally on the right page.

Cut a 4 in. (10 cm) strip from a transparency sheet and attach on the left side of the left page. Attach the remaining piece of transparency on the right side of the right page.

Title

Crumple a piece of metal foil and then unfold. Thread black fibers through holes in the top of letter charms to make up title. Attach the letter charms to the metal foil. Use strong adhesive or glue dots to attach the foil to the top right of the left background page.

Photo mounts

Mount photographs onto white card and trim an even border. Mount once again onto dark gray card and cut a double mount.

Finishing touches

Make a swingbook following the step-by-step instructions and attach to the top right of the right page. Attach mounted photographs and finish with a word charm mounted onto dark gray card.

Making a Swingbook

1 Cut four pieces of cardstock 4 in. x 3½ in. (10 cm x 9 cm). Turn over and measure and mark a line ½ in. (13 mm) along one long edge.

2 Draw four lines at 1 in. (2.5 cm) intervals along the pencil line toward the edge.

3 Select a different 1 in. (2.5 cm) on each card to be the tab and cut away the ½ in. (13 mm) strip of excess card.

4 Secure a brad to the center of each tab.

5 Pierce a hole in one corner of each of the cards opposite the tabs.

6 Secure the cards together loosely with a large brad.

City Limits

Designer: Dawn Inskip

MATERIALS

Pale yellow
   cardstock
Stitch effect paper
Brown patterned
   paper
Plain paper
Alphabet stickers
Bookplate/label
   holder
Box clasp
Metal corners
Brads
Small tags

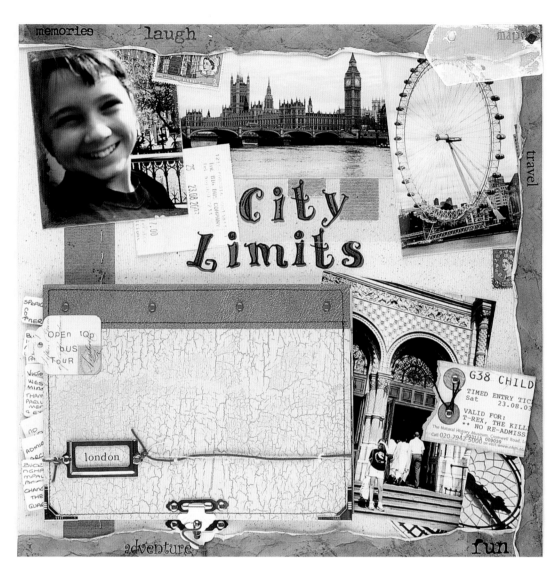

This is a record of a trip to London. Extra space has been created by using a mini-album on the page.

Instructions

Use a sheet of pale yellow card as the main background. Cut a strip of stitched effect paper and adhere to the left side of the background. Tear, curl, and chalk strips of brown patterned paper and attach to the edges of the background to create a border. Add stickers and rub-ons to the border.

Photo mounts

Sand the edges of all the photographs with fine-grade sandpaper, and adhere to the background with adhesive, tucking some of them under the edges of the curled border.

Mini-album

Create a mini-album by cutting two pieces of card 7 in. x 5 in. (18 cm x 13 cm) for the covers. Cover the card with patterned paper, ensuring that the corners are sharp and neat.

Fold a 7 in. x 5 in. (18 cm x 13 cm) strip of plain paper in a concertina every ½ in. (13 mm) along the longer side. Attach the folded paper to the inside edges of each cover. Cut a 7 in. x 3 in. (18 cm x 7.5 cm) strip of contrasting paper and stick this to the front edge of one cover, over the concertina folds. Wrap it around the rear cover and adhere. Finish by stitching around the front cover, adding brads, a bookplate, and decorative corners.

Carly and I finally got to London – after HD on PC went pear-shaped the previous day! Got an early train from Hitchin, Travel Card cost 12 pounds for me and 1 pound for – a bargain. On top of that, parking at Hitchin station was free.

Took our time on the Underground, so no chance of getting ourselves lost. Headed for the Natural History Museum and Dinosaur exhibit – goes without saying! The to T-Rex The Killer Question exhibit – was T-Rex a Scavenger, Hunter or both, we decided he was both. After a few more exhibits we left to 'do' an open-top bus tour.

Caught Underground to Trafalgar Square and hopped on a bus – 17 pounds for me and 8 pounds for Carly. Our cockney tour guide was very informative and hilarious – definitely had the gift of the gab – got Carly helping him out too. Saw things we'd not noticed before and our guide pointed out a million and one things not on the map. Weather was glorious, which was just as well and Carly and I only dressed in shorts!

The tour took us past Admiralty Arch and The Mall, Horse-guards Parade, Downing Street, Parliament and Big Ben. As we crossed the Thames, got an awesome view of The London Eye. On past Waterloo Station and Euro-tunnel train was in the station. Rambled on past Covent Garden, Fleet Street, St Pauls and Tower Bridge. A great view of the moat and vast grounds of the Tower of London – interesting viewing from a different perspective. Back along the Thames and on to Buckingham Palace and Marble Arch – where we had to change buses.

Got off again at Regent Street to visit Hamleys and drooled at the Steiff Bears. Underground back to Kings Cross and home – exhausted What a day we had, and wondered why we didn't do it more often

With the book open, you can see that a mini-album is perfect for holding additional photographs and journaling without cluttering the page.

Finishing touches

Adhere the mini-album to the page, attaching a decorative closure or box clasp to keep the book closed. Add small tags to the left edge of each photo for journaling. Add a title using stickers and memorabilia as you wish.

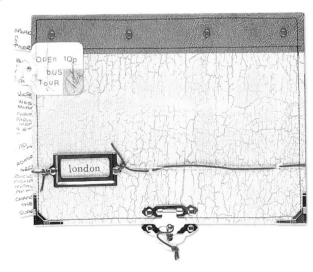

At the Waterhole
Designer: Natalie O'Shea
Pick out the colors in your
photograph and use these
for your accent colors.

My Kind of Town

Designer: Mandy Webb

MATERIALS

Plain cardstock
Patterned paper
Foam stamps
Acrylic paint
Rub-on lettering
Square punch
Snaps

Instructions

Use a patterned paper as the main background. Using foam stamps and acrylic paint, stamp a title directly onto the background down one side. Set aside to allow the paint to dry.

Photo mount

Mount the focal point photograph onto plain cardstock and trim a narrow border. Attach to the background using contrasting colored snaps.

Use a square punch to cut-out a variety of background images from photographs, each the same shape and size. Mount these onto plain cardstock, leaving a small border around each image. Attach the strip of pictures to the background at the top of the layout.

Finishing touches

Use rub-on lettering to add journaling directly onto the background. Use decorative snaps to add color and interest to the photo mounts.

Try using a punch to create evenly sized pictures that can be combined in a strip for a clean, consistent look.

Baby

Babies are precious, so preserve your memories of this short time by creating a special baby album.

My Son

I wish you
the strength to
face challenges with
confidence...
along with the
wisdom to
choose your
battles
carefully...
I wish you
adventure on
your journey and
may you always
stop to help
someone along
the way...
Listen to
your heart
and take risks
carefully...
Remember
how much
you are loved...
I am so proud
of you!

Let Him Sleep
Designer: Alison McGovern

How quickly the babies in our lives grow and change. In the blink of an eye it seems they are walking, talking, and leaving babyhood behind. You can never seem to take too many pictures of a baby, every day brings new discoveries and developments that should be recorded. Ensure that your journaling includes dates, times, weights, places, and people to create a scrapbook that will replace the baby book as a meaningful record of these first months. The soft-focus photograph and wording on this page are created by printing over canvas on a computer printer (see page 116).

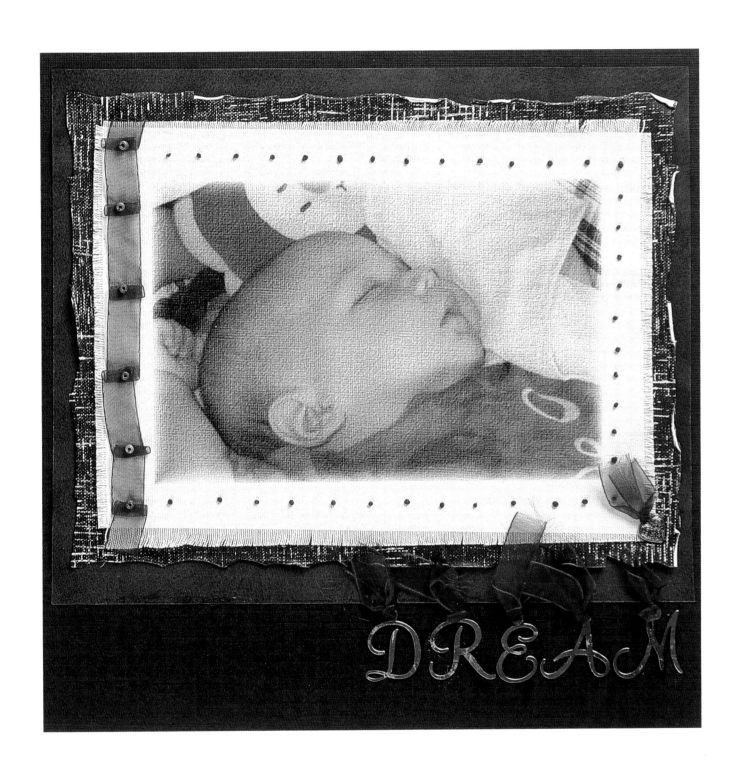

DREAM

Making "Let Him Sleep"

Printing a photograph onto canvas gives this focal point picture a soft finish that is perfect for a baby.

MATERIALS

Black cardstock

Canvas

Red and black
  patterned papers

Organza ribbon

Eyelet letters

Heart charm

Embroidery floss

Beads

Needle and thread

Instructions

Use black cardstock for the main backgrounds of both sides of the design. Trim 1 in. (2.5 cm) from two adjacent sides of the red patterned paper and attach this centrally onto the black card for the left page.

Photo mounts

Tear a sheet of black patterned paper into a rectangle measuring 10 in. x 6 in. (25.5 cm x 15 cm) and three further 4 in. (10 cm) squares. Dampen the edges of each piece of black paper and roll the torn edge. Leave to dry.

Print the photograph and phrases onto the canvas following the step-by-step instructions below. Attach the photo and phrase strips to the mounts using embroidery floss. Try a variety of stitches to add interest and texture to the design. Attach the mounted photo and phrases to the left page of the design.

Tear a photo mount 11 in. x 9 in. (28 cm x 23 cm) from a further sheet of black patterned paper and roll the edges as before. Print a large focal point picture onto canvas with a generous border.

Attach the photo to the black rolled mount using French knots (see page 75). Mount onto an 11 in. x 9 1/2 in. (28 cm x 24 cm) mount cut from red patterned paper. Attach to the right page of the design.

Finishing touches

Attach a length of organza ribbon down one side of the focal point picture on the right page. Make small pleats at 1 in. (2.5 cm) intervals and secure these in place by attaching a bead with a needle and thread.

Cut a further 12 in. (30.5 cm) of organza ribbon and tie three knots at intervals along the length. Attach this to the left page of the design. Tie short lengths of ribbon through each of the eyelet letters and the heart charm. and attach to the right page of the layout.

Printing on canvas

1 Print a guide sheet of your designs onto regular printer paper and cut a piece of canvas the correct size.

2 Attach a piece of canvas over the printed design, leaving approximately 3/4 in. (2 cm) border. Use artist's tape or repositionable mount adhesive.

3 Place into the printer paper tray and print again before removing the printed canvas from the paper guide sheet.

4 Fray the edges of the canvas pieces by gently pulling the threads at the sides. If the threads are difficult to get hold of, tease them out with a sharp pin or needle.

5 Sew the printed designs onto paper mounts using a variety of stitches for added interest and texture.

6 Use this technique to create a narrative on your page by repeating phrases or making a sentence.

Father's Pride

Designer: Mandy Webb

A strong black and white photograph with a printed transparency laid over the top, creates a page that captures the father-son bond.

Instructions

Use a sheet of plain cardstock as the main background and cover with a sheet of patterned vellum.

Cut a 14 in. (35.5 cm) length of cream mesh and thread two lengths narrow ribbon along the long edges. Attach the mesh along the left side of the background, folding the ends onto the reverse before securing.

Photo mount

Mount a large single photograph onto cream cardstock and trim a narrow border along the top, bottom and right side. Trim a 2 in. (5 cm) wide border along the left side of the photograph.

Trim the acetate to cover the mounted photograph. Attach the acetate with a small amount of adhesive in the top right and bottom left corners. Cover the adhesive with buttons.

Attach the mounted photograph to the background, overlapping the mesh border.

Finishing touches

Mount the vellum quote onto cardstock and trim. Edge the top and bottom of the quote with ribbon and attach to the upper right side of the background. Add buttons to decorate.

Nine-month Journey

Designer: Dawn Inskip

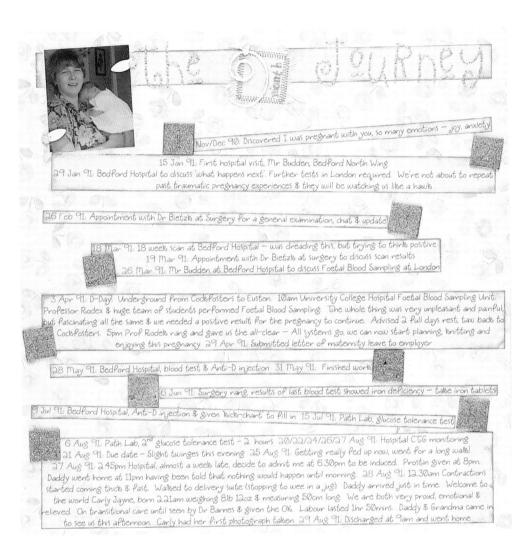

MATERIALS

Patterned paper

Ink pads

Embossing
   powder

Alphabet stamps

Metal number tiles

Photo anchors

Spiral clip

Embroidery floss

Sewing thread

Ribbon

Brads

Mulberry paper

Instructions

Use a sheet of patterned paper as the main background. Computer generate journaling onto a co-ordinating mulberry paper and cut this into strips. Ink the edges of each strip and adhere these to the background varying the position and angle of each.

Title

Cut another strip of co-ordinating patterned paper for the title block. Ink the edges and adhere to the top of the page. Print out a title onto scrap paper. Place the printed title over the title block and carefully prick evenly spaced holes tracing the lettering. Remove the printed title and stitch through the holes with thread. Tear a 1¼ in. (3 cm) square from mulberry paper and mount onto a 1 in. (2.5 cm) square of patterned paper to strengthen it. Use a sewing machine to stitch around the square before stamping part of the title along one edge. Adhere to the title strip. Attach a small photograph to one side of the title strip with photo anchors and brads.

Finishing touches

Coat metal numerals with ink and apply embossing powder. Set with a heat gun before attaching the relevant numbers to the edges of the journaling strips with a strong adhesive. Manipulate a spiral clip to form the number "9". Tie a knot with ribbon at the top of the "9" and attach to the mulberry square.

Scrapbook pages can be created, even when there are no photographs of the event. Here, journaling records the nine months of pregnancy.

Precious

Designer: Sarah Mason

This is another great example of a strong baby layout using simple black and white photography against a soft-colored background to full effect.

A IS FOR ANNABEL

PRECIOUS

Wedding

Keep your treasured memories in pristine
condition with archival quality materials
to prevent deterioration.

Forever

Designer: Alison McGovern

Flowers and weddings are a perfect combination. A crackle glaze paint effect used over a strong floral paper, produces a soft, cloudy finish. Dried rosebuds are the perfect embellishment for this romantic page.

Making "Forever"

Although there is certain to be an official photographer at a wedding, it is often the guests who take the best shots. Candid and more relaxed pictures can be captured in the seconds after the official posed shot has been taken. Formal pictures can make wonderful scrapbook pages but the relaxed shot will capture the real personalities of the bride and groom. Try mixing both styles of picture for pages that gather together the formality and fun of this special day.

Think about saving items such as the Order of Service, menu, and place cards as these are unique to the occasion and can all be incorporated into your scrapbook pages.

You can even dry the flowers from the bouquets and decorations. If you don't manage to collect some confetti or mementos from the day, you can always cheat and buy some after the event to create the same effect.

MATERIALS

Plain card
Patterned paper
Dried rosebuds
Ribbon
Acrylic paint
Crackle glaze
Foam stamps

Instructions

Rub an ink pad around the outside edges of two sheets of plain colored cardstock to produce a shabby, uneven tinted edge. Use these as the main background.

Crackle glazing

Trim 1½ in. (4 cm) from two adjacent sides of two sheets of patterned paper. Paint and crackle these sheets of paper following the step-by-step instructions opposite.

Wrap two lengths of ribbon around one sheet of crackle-painted paper, securing the ends on the reverse. Attach both sheets of paper centrally onto the plain inked card.

Photo mounts

Mount a focal point photograph onto plain cardstock and trim an even border. Mount once again onto patterned paper and trim a wide border.

Mount smaller photographs directly onto patterned paper and trim ¾ in. (2 cm) borders.

Attach the small photographs onto the ribboned side of the background. Attach the focal point photo centrally onto the remaining background sheet.

Finishing touches

Attach rosebuds around two sides of the focal point photo and across the bottom of the ribboned page.

Attach single rosebuds to each small photograph. Gather three rosebuds together and attach to the bottom left of the focal point side of the design.

Use foam stamps to create a title under the focal point picture. Tie a large ribbon bow and adhere to the top left corner of the focal point picture.

Making a crackle-glazed page

1 Using wide brush strokes, paint a base color over the paper to be crackled. Set aside and leave to dry.

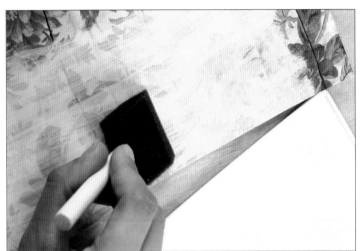

2 When the paint is completely dry, apply a thin coat of crackle glaze using a paintbrush or sponge. When almost dry, paint on a second coat of paint in one direction only.

3 As the paint dries it will react with the underlying layers causing cracks. Once dry, the paint surface can be distressed further with fine sandpaper.

4 The finished effect gives a wonderfully soft, aged finish, perfect for a wedding page.

Happily Ever After

Designer: Alison Docherty

MATERIALS

Plain cardstock

Contrasting
   cardstock

Patterned paper

Word charm

Beads

Hole punch

Ink pad

Wire

Eyelets

Fabric flowers

Brad

Rub-on words

Wire and beads threaded through eyelets create a sophisticated border. A monochromatic color palette keeps the focus on the photographs.

Instructions

Use a sheet of plain cardstock as the main background. Trim a sheet of contrasting card to 11 in. x 11 in. (28 cm x 28 cm) and attach to the center of the background. Trim a strip of patterned paper 12 in. x 3½ in. (30.5 cm x 9 cm) and adhere to the right side of the background.

Measure and mark at regular intervals along the join between the patterned paper and the background. Punch holes for eyelets at alternate marks on each side of the join, creating a zig-zag pattern. Set eyelets in each hole.

Photo mount

Mount photographs onto plain cardstock and trim an even border. Rub an ink pad lightly around the edges of each photo mount to highlight. Attach the mounted photographs to the background.

Finishing touches

Pass wire through the eyelets and thread on beads in co-ordinating colors. Continue to create a zig-zag of beads and secure the wire ends on the reverse.

Attach a word charm onto cardstock and ink the edges before adhering to the background. Attach fabric flowers together using a brad and adhere to the background using a adhesive dot. Use rub-on words or lettering to create a title.

New Beginnings

Designer: Natalie O'Shea

to have and to hold

MATERIALS

Plain card
Contrasting card in
    three colors
Craft knife
Cutting mat
Word charm
Silk fabric

Instructions

Use a plain color of cardstock for the main background.

Photo mount

Mount a photograph onto plain card and trim a narrow, even border. Mount again onto contrasting card and trim a narrow border. Mount once again onto silk fabric and cut a wide border. Mount this finally onto cardstock with a narrow border.

Attach the mounted photograph to the right side of the background.

Finishing touches

Print the title text in reverse on the wrong side of plain cardstock. Use a craft knife and glass cutting mat to cut out the title before attaching this to the left side of the background.

Attach a word charm to the top left of the background.

A highly decorative title, handcut from plain cardstock, makes a stunning page – perfect for the beginning of a wedding album.

Special Occasions

There are usually pictures of the important moments in our lives, but how often do we do something with them?

First Bike

Designer: Alison McGovern

These are the times when we make the effort to take along our cameras, but choosing the best shots can be hard. Be honest, and choose the pictures that capture the occasion and discard any that are out of focus or cut off people's heads. Special occasions sometimes mean lots of cameras and you may find great pictures were taken by someone else, so ask for copies to be sure you have the widest choice.

Making "First Bike"

Instructions

Chalks can be used in combination with stamps and watermark inkpads to create shaded borders and titles. Selecting a color from the patterned paper produces a co-ordinated palette.

Background

Use purple cardstock as the main background. Trim ½ in. (13 mm) from the top and right edges of two sheets of patterned paper and attach these centrally onto both backgrounds. Attach purple brads through each corner.

Photo mounts

Cut green cardstock to 10 in. x 7 in. (25.5 cm x 18 cm) and highlight the edges using colored chalks. Attach this at an angle on the right page. Adhere photographs overlapping this mount and the background paper.

Cut a mount for a main photograph from purple cardstock, leaving a ½ in. (13 mm) border. Highlight the edges of the mount with chalk. Attach to the center of the left page at an angle.

Title

Use foam stamps and clear embossing ink to stamp a title directly onto the background. Following the steps opposite, apply chalk over the clear ink until the required depth of color is achieved.

Use license plate stickers to create a title and attach to the second page.

Chalk enhancement

Using a paintbrush lightly paint the edge of your photo mat with a chalk enhancer. Using the applicator provided, or a cotton bud, apply chalk directly onto the chalk enhancer. The chalk will now appear to be more of a watercolor medium than a chalked line.

Finishing touches

Use the chalk enhancement technique above to add color to the acrylic alphabet letters before attaching them to both pages as desired. Add a canvas phrase and use a label maker to add journaling.

Use rub-on letters and alphabet stickers to add journaling to the photo mounts. Mount a small photo inside a frame charm and attach to the top of the left page using a brad. Attach a bottle cap to the corner of the chalked paper mount.

Resist chalking

1 Stamp on the paper with your chosen stamp using a resist, or watermark type, inkpad.

2 Using either the chalk applicator provided or a cotton bud, lightly sweep chalk over the image until the required effect is achieved. The wet ink "picks up" the chalk particles and now shows the image stamped "in chalk."

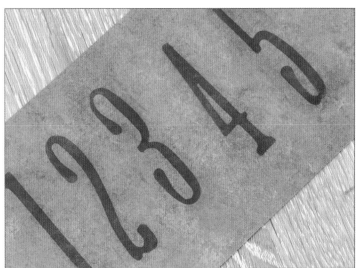

3 Dust off any remaining chalk from around the image with a ball of cotton batting (cotton wool), taking care not to cause smudging.

4 Once the background has been wiped clean of chalk dust, the letters or numbers will stand out clearly.

Turning Two

Designer: Sarah Mason

MATERIALS

Plain cardstock
Patterned paper
Metal mesh
Cork
Woven label
Alphabet stickers
Brads
Conchos

Create your own embellishments using mesh and stencils for a unique and personal touch.

Instructions

Use a sheet of blue cardstock for the main background. Cut a 10 in. x 5 in. (25.5 cm x 13 cm) strip of co-ordinating blue card and attach horizontally across the upper part of the background.

Cut a 6 in. x 11½ in. (15 cm x 29 cm) strip of patterned paper and attach this vertically to the right of the background.

Cut a triangle of metal mesh and attach to the top right corner of the design.

Photo mounts

Mount photographs onto white card and trim an even border. Attach photographs to the background, adhering a triangle of cork under the top right corner of one photo.

Title

Use a number stencil to cut a shape out from a square of metal mesh. Highlight the cut edges of the metal with a black permanent marker. Cut a square of cork smaller than the mesh and place under the number. Secure the mesh to the cork using brads.

Create a title with individual letter stickers.

Finishing touches

Add a fabric label, studs, and conchos to complete the design. The conchos are filled with diamond glaze to give them extra dimension. See "Using Glazes" on page 34.

Unforgettable

Designer: Dawn Inskip

Instructions

Use a light gray cardstock as the main background. Tear and chalk a patterned paper into strips and layer this over the background.

Cut a length of self-adhesive mesh and swipe with a clear embossing pad. Sprinkle with platinum, copper, gold, and black embossing powders before heat setting. Adhere the mesh across the background. Randomly adhere sand to the torn edges of the background strips and mesh. Stitch a large hook and eye fastener to one side of a torn strip.

Photo mount

Cut a strip of patterned paper 1 in. (2.5 cm) wide along the height of the photo. Fold a narrow strip along the length and tuck this behind one end of the photo, secure on the reverse. Tear the front edge of the patterned paper before attaching this in place on the front of the picture. Wrap a length of ribbon around the patterned paper and decorate with a scrap of fabric and a fancy button. Attach the mounted photograph centrally on the design.

Title

Computer-print a title onto a sheet of transparency. While the ink is still wet, apply silver embossing powder and set with a heat gun. Attach the transparency across the top of the page with brads and metal photo corners.

Finishing touches

Load a label maker with dark gray patterned paper and emboss your journaling. Rub the raised print with fine-grade sandpaper before attaching to the lower edge of the page. Add a decorative frame mounted over metal numerals, charms, and memorabilia all hung from a hook fastener secured to the page.

Try using a cardstock or paper with a white core, together with a label marker, to produce one-of-a-kind personal journaling strips.

1/06

Total **Scrapbooking**